Misdeeds by the Misguided

Jerry ~ Enjoy your own Misdeeds!

Jude Brogan

Jude Brogan

DEDICATION

To my family—Mike, Reggie, Becky, Shannon, and Mary Ann—you are the true north that keeps me honest. Thank you for giving me endless material to use, not to mention not minding me splashing our exploits in front of God and country. Special thanks to Mama Bear for believing I could do this, telling me I could do this, and helping me do this.

I started out many, many years ago thinking I would write a book, maybe self-published, maybe a national best-seller (yeah, right!). I scrapped more than a dozen attempts at The Great American Novel; I just didn't have the attention span to delve into even a fictional person's life that much. So, I thought maybe I could write humor, like Erma Bombeck. The trouble with that was that life isn't always funny. Sometimes it's sad, frustrating, bizarre, and just plain dull. Then I thought I would be deeply philosophical, like Robert Fulgham. The trouble with that was that I was too busy surviving on a day-to-day basis to be philosophical.

So I decided to write as just plain me, an average person who has had some funny things happen, has had some sad things happen, and hasn't had anything happen at all; probably much the same as most of you. If I manage to create laughter, that's good. If all I manage to do is share part of my life and how I view it, I guess that's not all bad either.

Because the book platform seemed unrealistic for me, I started a blog instead which has been more fun than I ever thought possible. However, the book idea never really went away, especially with blog readers asking me if or when I was going to turn the blog into a book.

So now I have come full circle and have turned the blog into a book.

Misdeeds by the Misguided is a look at the life and times of me, my family, and my friends. It's about farming, gardening, traveling, and trying to make sense out of the world around us. I really hope you enjoy reading what I so much enjoyed writing.

While all of these episodes are true, I have taken the creative liberty of using nicknames for those I write about most: my husband (Captain), my son (Young Man), my daughter (Princess), my daughter-in-law (Mama Bear), and my granddaughter (Cubby). While I don't mind, and actually enjoy, being the center of attention, not everyone I know feels the same way. The relationships aren't relative anyway. It's the lesson or insight behind the story that is important.

CONTENTS

ACKNOWLEDGMENTS

I could never have gotten this book to publication without the help of a lot of people. To my proofreading posse, thank you for being vigilant about verbs, crazy about commas, and precise about pronouns! To my ingenious illustrator, my deepest gratitude for "nailing" the artwork. To my Photoshop fairy, thank you for getting the right illustration in the right place! To my scripture seekers, your contributions were a Godsend. To every single person I asked for help from page numbering to line spacing, you guys rock!

MOM-ISMS

There is a supernatural phenomenon that occurs in every mother's psyche that we are afraid to talk about for fear of being labeled a lunatic. However, since misery loves company and there is safety in numbers, I'll go first.

As soon as our children were born, my mother took up residence inside my brain; at least that part of my brain that controls my speech.

I didn't become alarmed after the first episode; I just chalked it up to a fluky coincidence. Young Man had a sucker in his mouth and was running through the house. I opened my mouth to deliver a new-millennium kind of speech about how inappropriate this was, but what came out was, "Don't run with that sucker in your mouth or you'll fall down and choke to death."

As soon as the words were out, I whipped around fully expecting to see my mother. Of course, she wasn't there, even though those were HER words—the same ones I swore I would never say.

The next time it happened, I was listening to Princess list what she wanted for Christmas. One item in particular that was obscenely expensive I flat-out refused to even consider. I was then treated to the full guilt trip, complete with basset-hound eyes and trembling lower lip accompanied by a howl of "So-and-so has one."

Again, the contemporary response I meant to say was replaced by, "Well I'm not so-and-so's mother; I'm your mother, and I said no."

Now, I'm all for mother-daughter bonding, but this was having Mom a little too close.

I brought the subject up to Captain, expecting a little sympathy for this terrible malady I was enduring. He just said, "What do you expect? You're a mom...don't ALL moms say that stuff?"

I don't know, I never asked. But I was sure no one else was suffering these symptoms. After all, there was no support group for this disease. I know, I looked it up in the phone book.

I might have survived this psychic invasion by sheer willpower if Young Man hadn't invited a friend over. I was listing the things that needed to be cleaned out or picked up before his friend came over. With one of those looks that only a child who is being punished with incredibly unintelligent parents can master, he said neither he nor his friend cared how the house looked.

An uneasy feeling crept over me as I recalled those words from my own childhood. Afraid to open my mouth, knowing what I was going to say, I still tried to get rational words out. However, my voice box and brain cells were once again commandeered by Mom. Wincing, I heard the words, "Well *I* care what the house looks like, so do it."

Now I knew I was in trouble. I sent the kids outside to play so I could sit down and think this through rationally. And it hit me like a bolt of lightning.

Those words have been spoken by moms for generations and will continue to be spoken for more generations. My own mother had used those admonitions quite successfully to raise three children (myself included) into responsible, mature adults (myself not included).

She had set an example I should be honored to follow with my own children. Besides, if I used these techniques on my own children, someday Princess would be having this same question of sanity going through her mind, and that would be more than worth my current anguish.

I gave in to a sudden impulse and yelled the most mom-like thing I could remember from my childhood. "When all that fighting results in someone getting hurt, don't come crying to me."

"She opens her mouth with wisdom, and the teaching of kindness is on her tongue." Proverbs 31:26

BUCKET LIST

Did you know there are 75 state parks in Minnesota? As much as camping has been a part of our lives since we got married, I did not know this until Captain and I put "visit every state park in Minnesota" on our bucket list, and I started researching.

Captain introduced me to the joys of tent camping about 30 years ago. Up to that point, I don't know as I knew what a tent was. My family was more the Holiday Inn kind of folks. Anyhoo, Captain's family camped frequently and had all the paraphernalia that went with it...Coleman stove, Coleman lantern, tents, sleeping bags, etc.

Camping was a good option for us when the kids were young because it was so much cheaper than a hotel and restaurants, plus it gave them all kinds of room to run around and burn off energy.

Ask one of them sometime about the cart-in site we stayed at in Frontenac State Park and then hiked 400 feet down to Lake Pepin. Apparently Captain was the only one who realized that we would also have to hike 400 feet almost straight back up to get back to the campsite!

Camping in state parks also let the kids learn some history of Minnesota and see some amazing sites like Gooseberry Falls and Split Rock Lighthouse.

The thing we like most about Minnesota state parks, other than the obvious nature aspect, is that every single one of them has excellent shower facilities. I don't mind cooking over an open fire, using a flashlight to get to the bathroom in the middle of the night, or sleeping on the ground. However, I refuse to do the sponge bath thing to clean up. I need my shower every day!

Since camping requires organization, I made up an Excel spreadsheet of things to pack from Advil to Ziploc bags. It still never fails that I forget something.

One time when we had Young Man and his favorite cousin, I forgot the rain fly for our tent. The boys' tent had a rain fly, so Captain spent the night in their tent. I ended up sleeping in the truck which resulted in my having laryngitis the rest of the trip, which the kids didn't mind because I couldn't yell at them that way!

Then there was the year we took the kids to the Black Hills the summer that Young Man graduated high school. Kind of a "last hurrah" as a family vacation. It was the last week in July in South Dakota, and we had to sleep in winter coats, hats, and mittens because it got down to 36 degrees the first two nights we were there. But, oh, the days were lovely!

I'm not sure about Princess, but I can see Young Man taking Mama Bear and Cubby there someday on vacation. Maybe not in a tent, though.

Our absolute favorite state park area is the North Shore. I told Captain once that I don't need to see the ocean...Lake Superior is grand enough! We have visited there a dozen times over the years, and there is always something new to explore and discover, along with returning to some treasured spots like Palisade Head, Gooseberry Falls, Tettegouche, and Grand Marais. Seeing the Pigeon River—with the United States on one side and Canada on the other side--is amazing.

This weekend, Captain and I are sneaking away for an overnight camping trip to Lake Sakatah State Park. We've been there before with some very good friends and enjoyed it immensely. It's only an hour away from home; there is fishing, hiking, biking, and you can rent a canoe. Should be an enjoyable time as long as I don't forget to pack something important!

"In his hand are the depths of the earth; the heights of the mountains are his also. The sea is his, for he made it, and his hands formed the dry land." Psalm 95:4-5

TODAY'S THOUGHTS

You wouldn't know it by seeing or talking to Captain, but he is the proud possessor of an impish streak a mile wide. To his great glee, he married the world's most gullible person. He enjoys seeing how much he can buffalo me, and (in the spirit of matrimonial harmony, of course) I let him have great success.

During a governor's campaign race many years ago, Captain was telling me that one of the candidates was accused of appearing nude at a swimming party, and the offered excuse for such vile behavior was that he was sleepwalking.

Because this sounded exactly like the sort of asinine thing a wanna-be public official would say, I believed Captain's account. That was my first mistake. My second mistake was in repeating it at card club the next night.

I went on and on about the increase of corruption in the government and the decline of morality in our elected officials until Captain interrupted me…to tell me he had made the whole thing up. Only the fact that there were four witnesses present kept him from being the guest of honor at a wake.

Captain not only uses verbal trickery, he is fond of the visual aspect of practical jokes too. Upon returning home from the grocery store once, I entered the kitchen only to spy a monstrous beetle-type bug on the counter.

Now, I pride myself on being largely unaffected by creepy crawlers, but I was pregnant at the time and given to uncharacteristic behavior. I dropped the four bags of groceries from my hands, slammed a bowl upside down over the bug, and ran screaming to the barn in search of a big, strong man to dispose of the big, ugly bug. Well, "ran" maybe isn't the right word; being 8-1/2 months pregnant, the best I could manage was a waddle.

I found Captain in the barn talking politics, religion, and women to a salesman. I ignored good manners and interrupted their conversation to inform Captain that our home had been invaded by a mutant alien life form roughly the size of New Jersey (hysteria and exaggeration being the prerogatives of mothers-to-be), and unless he wanted this particular woman to give him a sermon he wouldn't soon forget, he had best consider himself elected to take care of said alien life form.

Trying to maintain any semblance of dignity after Captain told me it was a plastic bug was futile. I simply waddled back to the house. Where I proceeded to bake that little plastic bug into Captain's apple pie.

Humorous—but not offensive or belittling—stories and the retelling of them are what make up the fabric of a family's history. It gives a sense of continuity and bonding. No one escapes having a tale told about them because everyone is human, and everyone makes mistakes. Blessed are those families with endless fabric to wrap themselves in love through the years!

"A joyful heart is good medicine..." Proverbs 17:22a

LAKE SAKATAH

We took the scenic route to Sakatah since we were in no real hurry, and this trip was supposed to be relaxing. We meandered through Kenyon on the way to Faribault and made a quick stop at Hardees for lunch.

We had to hit the Walmart across the street because our Coleman lantern hasn't worked the last three or four times we've tried it, so we decided to pick up a battery operated lantern instead. While we were cruising up and down the sporting goods aisles, it hit me what I had forgotten to pack...camp chairs. Lucky for us, there were some on sale! Loaded with the last of our essentials, including a new book for each of us, we went on to get checked into the park.

When we got to our site and started unloading, it only took two minutes to realize that the mosquitoes outnumbered us 1000 to 1 and we needed ammunition. We didn't even finish putting up the tent; instead it was back in the truck to drive into Waterville, two miles down the road. Pondered stopping at a Casey's convenience store but decided to check out main street to see if there might be a hardware store.

Jackpot two blocks down...Hardware Hank! I love hardware stores; they aren't just for men anymore, my friends! I would say this particular store has been owned and operated by the same person/family for decades.

It was one of those old main street stores where the aisles are so close together, if two people are in the same aisle, they are standing in sin. But let me say, if he didn't have what you were looking for, you probably didn't need it. And such a friendly, helpful, and delightful elderly man was running the store! He was genuinely interested in what we needed, why, and where we were from. There was even a little "free" table of stuff out on the sidewalk, so I picked up a little book for Cubby.

Armed with our Yard Guard, we returned to camp and went to war. After dispensing two-thirds of the can over as much of the site as we could, we went back to setting up camp and then decided to explore.

We walked down the main road toward the showers, then detoured through a different "loop" that had more campers and RVs than tents. One family had a rousing bean bag tournament going on, and the pre-teen boy was kicking butt! I am pretty sure that is because he was the only participant under legal drinking age...but I could be wrong about that. No matter, they were having fun as family and friends, and I can appreciate that.

After that, we decided to walk down to the boat launch and fishing pier area, but after maybe 500 yards, we turned back due to swarms of mosquitoes. I even slapped one on the side of my head so hard I made my ears ring! Darn things.

Somehow when we are camping, we are both asleep in the camp chairs by 9:00 while at home, it is usually 11:00 or later when we finally go to bed. Must be the fresh air and starlight.

Anyway, in the tent, I was just getting to sleep...you know that floaty, dreamy, all-is-well state right before you get to sleep? Something came crashing into the tent that sent me right into Chicken Little mode. My mind ran the gamut from psycho squirrel to Bigfoot (don't judge; childhood fears are REAL) to...what's the name of the stupid dinosaur that used to routinely stomp all over Japan in the movies...whatever.

When a second something came crashing into the tent, I remembered that the tent was pitched directly underneath a walnut tree, and we were being bombed periodically. Whew...better than a psycho squirrel! I snuggled in and went to sleep.

The next thing that woke me up was rain pattering on the tent. Thank heavens I remembered the rain fly this time or it would have been ugly. As it was, we were nice and cozy right where we were!

Of course, just before dawn, I needed to...ummm...use the facilities. Except the facilities were way down at the end of the loop and sort of a long walk. In the dark. By myself.

Yeah, yeah, yeah. I know I said I could put up with walking to a bathroom...just not in the dark. Remember the immediate thoughts of....man, WHAT was that dinosaur's name?!?! Anyway, the fear goes back to some brainless babysitter when I was a kid who let me watch some horror movie about lizard people. My fear of the dark has stayed with me ever since, making predawn trips to porta potties a dilemma.

I could wake up Captain, but that just seemed rude since he was sleeping so peacefully. Wait a minute, why are his feet in my face when his face was in my face when we went to sleep? He turned himself around apparently. Neither here nor there.

I toss and turn for a while hoping maybe I'm mistaken and I only *think* I need to pee. Toss, turn, toss. Nope, I need to pee. Then I heard the birds singing, so dawn must be breaking. Pretty sure Bigfoot hotfoots it back to the hills during the day. Probably safe to venture out. Suffice it to say, the new battery operated lantern kept all fears at bay!

We both waited until the sun was full up to crawl out of the tent. I headed for the showers and Captain hung out at camp. When I pack for camping and I contemplate toiletries, I always think to myself "It's camping...who's gonna care what I look like?" So I only pack shampoo, soap, and toothpaste. I regret it every single time when I have no conditioner, no comb, and no hair ties. Psycho squirrels got nothing on me with just-been-showered hair.

The rain seemed to have quadrupled the skeeter population, so I refused to make breakfast in camp. Besides, we hadn't been prepared for the rain so everything from firewood to food was soaked. Perkins, here we come!

Rejuvenated by food that someone else cooked and served, we returned to camp to break down and head out. Rolling up the tent was a muddy mess, and I couldn't get the sleeping bags rezipped. Tossed it all in the back of the truck helter skelter and got the hell out of dodge.

On the way home, we stopped at Big Woods State Park outside of Nerstrand, also a repeat trip for us, but they have a waterfalls area a short hike from the picnic area. Memo to anyone else visiting Hidden Falls...take the trail from the campground down to the falls and the trail to the picnic area up from the falls. If you do it the other way around, you will be ready to die. Or maybe you are in better shape than I am. Just saying.

Mishaps, mistakes, and--you guessed it--misdeeds were all words of the weekend. Even though it was less than 24 hours, it's always good to get away. But, boy oh boy, was it nice to come home again!

"The steadfast love of the Lord never ceases; his mercies never come to an end; they are new every morning; great is your faithfulness." Lamentations 3:22-23

GARDEN FEVER

Robert Bridges, an English poet from the early 1900s, once said "If odour were visible, like colour is, I would see the summer garden in rainbow clouds."

I don't know if he meant flower gardens or vegetable gardens, but either way, it's a nice visual.

My mom had a huge garden when we were growing up. I hated it. Every part of it. Planting, weeding, harvesting, preserving, eating. No thank you.

That's why it is surprising that now, in my fourth decade of life, I love almost all aspects of gardening. Except weeding; I just can't make that one a positive thing no matter how I twist it around. At best, it is a necessary evil. At worst, it is the ruination of a perfectly good day.

But I digress.

Planting...how exciting to imagine the potential of summer bounty when putting plants and seeds in the dirt. I have become something of a fanatic about flower gardening. I spend days to weeks planning the layout of all my flower pots or containers (and I have two dozen pots/containers...no joke). Young Man once asked me why I "keep putting crap in the yard to mow around." Because it makes me happy, my friend!

One of those containers is a whiskey barrel purchased from Menards by Captain and the kids (that sort of sounds like a breakfast cereal, doesn't it) for me for Mother's Day one year.

I filled it with steer yard dirt (that's "compost" to all of you non-farm folks) and plunked a daisy and petunias in it. They grew to astronomical proportions. The next year, it was dusty millers...again, mutant growth. For a couple of years after that, it was sweet potato vines that eventually completely covered the barrel. I don't know what's in that dirt (actually I do), but I've been tempted a couple of times to have Captain's agronomist soil sample it and tell me what the magic ingredient is. This year, I planted flowering kale, ageratum, and a green spiky plant.

Each year when I am planning the annuals, I always leave one container as the "mystery plant" spot. I like to try one new plant each year, just to see what's what. There have been hits and misses there (memo to me, snapdragons don't do well for me), but I learn something every year.

The vegetable garden is pretty standard with several varieties of tomatoes, swiss chard, green beans, squash, zucchini, eggplant, cucumbers, and lettuce. Captain doesn't like it when his mom and I plant the rows of seeds because they "aren't straight enough." Well geez, who cares? We are just getting more product per square inch doing it our way. Nope, not good enough. He hauls out the string and posts so he can plant a straight row. Whatever...it makes him happy.

In the early weeks after planting the garden, we check it almost daily, as if there is magic whisky barrel dirt out there that will makes Jack's beanstalk grow. By the time stuff is actually starting to ripen, the weeds are so out of control that it's hard to find the produce. Princess always complained when we made her pick green beans about "whose dumb idea was it to make the bean the same color as the vines and leaves so that the beans are easy to miss." Talk to God, sweetie, it was His idea.

My first foray into preserving was a salsa recipe from my good friend, Mae, and I still use it to this day. For a couple of years, I tried the Mrs. Wages salsa mix instead because it was quicker, but I soon went back to the homemade recipe because it was better. So often, good things are worth the extra time and effort.

After that, I expanded my horizons into pizza sauce and pasta sauce. As in dozens of pints of both each year, not to mention the dozens of pints of salsa and quarts of plain stewed tomatoes. That is a lot of work the old fashioned way of blanching, peeling, and quartering the tomatoes. I finally invested in a Sauce Master at Hardware Hank. What used to take hours now took just minutes. The machine removes the peels, cores, and seeds with just the turn of a crank. Ingenious!

Another good friend of mine did a lot of pressure canning of vegetables, and after having home canned green beans at their house one evening, Captain said I should get one also because, "Damn, those were better than anything you buy in the store." The first time I used the pressure cooker, I was such a nervous wreck about possibly blowing up the house, I texted my friend every 30 seconds to double check I was doing it right. Apparently I was, because that year I had 35 pints to tide us over the winter. Now I also do pints of vegetable soup. My next trick is going to be canning some stew meat. We'll see how that goes.

I also used to use Mrs. Wages Dill Pickle mix, but the flavor just wasn't quite right. I did some the next year using the Ball Canning Book recipe, which were better, but still not just right. Then I accidentally stumbled upon a recipe on the internet that did not call for pickling spice...mainly because I was out of pickling spice at the time I needed to put up pickles. Oh. My. Goodness. Those were the best pickles I've ever made or tasted. Since I don't have my own patch of dill, I am going to a friend's house to get some dill so I can make some awesome pickles to last us through the winter!

In your life's garden, I hope you have many beautiful blooms, few weeds, and a bountiful harvest of rainbow clouds!

"He makes grass grow for the cattle, and plants for people to cultivate—bringing forth food from the earth." Psalm 104:14

4-H MEMORIES

Tonight I am going to the fair to watch some friends' grandchildren show cattle in the novice group of the open class Holstein show. It will be like old home week because Captain and I were both 4-H members, and we both showed dairy cattle. In fact, that's how we met.

I showed cattle because my baby brother did, although he was *into* it and I was only in it for the socialization aspect. I competed for four or five years and never got a state fair trip. I'm not sure I ever even got a blue ribbon. Doesn't matter, because I got better stuff.

Being in 4-H teaches you about hard work. It doesn't matter if your project is an animal, a pie, a dress, a photograph, vegetables, or a demonstration. You can't just throw it together the night before the fair starts. It takes practice, practice, practice. Days, weeks, months of practice.

I remember doing posters every year for Junior Leadership. Being a fly by the seat of my pants kind of person, I always thought that leave it to the end thing would work. Lucky for me, my mom was smarter than that. I learned a few essentials from her. Have a plan, make a template, use a pencil first. Whereas I would have just started writing or coloring on the poster board, Mom made sure I drew straight lines for the lettering, centered the focal image, and used stencils for the lettering. My theory was always "It's good enough" while Mom's was "It can be better." If I earned a blue ribbon, it was thanks to Mom. I also learned to strive for more than just "good enough."

In 4-H, you learn how to do paperwork. Many projects, particularly the livestock projects, involve detailed records of how much the animal is fed and what that cost, what the vet costs were, what the animal's production was, and what that was worth. Other projects also require detailed explanations of costs, materials, and time spent. Those records are judged at the county and state levels for accuracy and neatness. A sub-lesson here is that 4-Hers learn the value of money and how to get the most bang for their buck.

One of the biggest things that a 4-H member learns that stays with them forever is public speaking. Every member, from Cloverbuds (kindergarten) to the graduating seniors, is required to give a demonstration in order to participate at the fair. This usually involves visual aids, an overview of the process involved in whatever project they are speaking about, and a finished project. There is a question and answer session from other members at the end of the demonstration. It is a terrifying experience for the majority of kids, but it is an elemental skill that is called upon later in life during interviews for things like scholarships and jobs. I've had more than one hiring manager tell me over the years that they can pick out which candidates have been in 4-H because their speaking ability is so much more advanced.

But the best thing about 4-H? Friendships that last for the rest of your life. Between me and Captain, I can count, at a minimum, two...no three...dozen of our friends that we met through 4-H. How freaking cool is that? Maybe you don't marry a fellow 4-Her like I did, but you never lose touch with your 4-H friends. When they get married, you're invited. When they have kids, you get an announcement. When there is a death in their family, you and other 4-H folks come out in droves for support. And vice versa.

Then the day comes when your kid and their kid are both standing in the show ring with a spring yearling, hoping for a ticket to the Great Minnesota Get Together. Their kid snags a trip and yours doesn't. I can guarantee that simultaneously you and your kid will turn to the winner (or parent) and say a sincere and heartfelt, "Congratulations, great job!"

"And let us not grow weary of doing good, for in due season we will reap, if we do not give up." Galatians 6:9

HAPPY FATHER-IN-LAW'S DAY

Got a text from Mama Bear this morning wishing Captain a Happy Father-in-Law day...how sweet! I didn't even know there was such a day.

I would say Happy FIL Day to Captain's dad, but we lost him in a drowning accident just over 8 years ago. I can't tell him, so I'll tell you.

He was a big man with a big heart. His life's motto was: "If something is in your way, go over it, under it, around it, or through it. Don't let it stop you." In other words, don't give up. We all pretty much still live by that rule.

He loved his family, had so many friends they can't be counted, and lived life the way he wanted to...fully.

His grandkids were his pride and joy. He always made sure before they'd part ways, he gave them "a big squeeze." The biggest treat for them was when Grampa would look at one of them and say, "Wanna run away today?" And off they'd go on an adventure.

One time he took Princess with him on a parts run to Heartland, Minnesota. Not such a long drive...unless you are a 9-year-old girl. Turns out the part Grampa needed wasn't at the dealer in Heartland, and to this day Princess talks about going to Heartland "for no good reason." But she got an ice cream cone out of the deal, so what's her beef?

Young Man was especially close to Grampa. They were buds. More like two peas in a pod, really. I see a lot of Captain's dad in Young Man, especially when he gets called on the carpet for something and puts on his puppy dog face and says, "The devil made me do it."

I truly believe that those who have passed are not truly gone. So I'll say it anyway, Happy Father-In-Law Day! He'll get the message.

"Honor your father and your mother, that your days may be long in the land that the LORD your God is giving you." Exodus 20:12

TIME, TALENT, AND TREASURE

Talent is a peculiar thing. You either have it or you don't. Sometimes you have degrees of it. There is one thing I excel at, and that is writing. Nailed that one. There are a lot of other things I am pretty good at but don't really shine. And there are some things I cannot do to save my soul.

Take cooking for instance. I love to cook, and I'm pretty good at it too. I've even managed to put 40 pounds on Captain since we got married. That brought him out of the "severely under-weight" BMI range and into borderline low-normal.

I was pretty proud of myself the day I turned out three loaves of homemade bread from scratch. No frozen bread dough or bread machine mix. Scratch. That takes talent, right?

So why can't I manage to make Rice Krispie bars? You tell me, and we might both know. This is the first baking project any beginner tries, but I can't do it after decades of trying. They either turn out like mortar bricks or they are soup. I follow the recipe down to the letter with the same bad result every time so I gave up on those.

Caramel corn is another one I have never mastered. Why should I, really, when Carroll's Corn serves the best caramel corn in town? The one time I tried making caramel corn, the dog wouldn't even eat it. What kind of rotten review is that? I've seen the things our dog eats, and it makes my caramel corn look like ambrosia.

Pre-packaged or single-serving grocery products cannot be found in our house. We buy the basics and make do. Or I try to copy the box mixes for this or that. I think I finally got the sour cream and cheddar potato thing down pat thanks to a crock pot recipe from Captain's mom. Who needs to buy the Rice-A-Roni Spanish rice mix when you can make Minute Rice and dump some salsa in it? Same outcome…major savings. I guess saving money is a talent as well, in its way.

This is why Captain does the grocery shopping now. All I was allowed to do for many years was cut the coupons and write the list. He started doing the shopping simply because going on a Saturday afternoon with two kids was beyond my capabilities. He could go at night after chores and be done in less time than it took me to get the kids out of their car seats.

Plus, he's better at it than I am. He does the whole coupon thing, store flyer, easy-saver-store-card, and comparison shopping of price-per-units. I don't have that kind of time or patience. Plus, while he's at the store doing the grocery thing, I'm at home with my feet up reading a good book. Getting the better end of the deal is the greatest talent of all, and I win!

If I wasn't adopted, I might have inherited my mother's talent for sewing and mending. Granted, those things can be learned, but there has to be an innate aptitude involved that I'm missing. When Young Man was smaller and would ruin the knees in his jeans faster than I could ruin a batch of caramel corn, my mom would take those jeans and patch them with the coolest things…a football on one knee and a baseball bat and ball on the other. He was the envy of every kid in his grade. I can't even manage those iron-on patches.

Princess' talent is fashion. I'm not sure where she got that because I know it wasn't from me. I do the basic colors of black, brown, or blue pants or skirts and toss on a colorful sweater, and I'm good to go. Or I thought I was until one day Princess gave me a critical up-and-down look and said, "You call *that* an outfit?" Let's see...bra, underwear, shirt, pants, hosiery, shoes. Yep, that's an outfit. Did I mention she was only 10 years old at the time?

And she likes to shop, which is another throwback mutation that did not come from me. I'm thinking my mother-in-law—who is the smartest dresser I know—passed those talents on to The Princess. They love to shop. I hate it. When I shop, I'm on a mission. I know what I want and what I'm willing to pay for it. If I don't find it on my first quick pass through the store, I leave and try another day. Those two will browse for hours, try on 57 different combinations of outfits, and they might come home with two that they liked, that fit, and they could afford. That's not talent; that's a disease.

Young Man is a throwback mutation as well. I'm pretty sure he was the Pied Piper in another lifetime. Little kids will follow him around like he's the answer to everything they've dreamed of. It's amazing. He can distract a cranky toddler until there is nothing but smiles. Older folks love him too because he is a rapt listener to all those "in my day" stories that get told at large family reunions. Listening is a talent I guess we could all work on more.

The three things we are supposed to contribute to this world are our time, talents, and treasures. I may not have a lot of talents, but my family is my biggest treasure of all time.

"As each has received a gift, use it to serve one another, as good stewards of God's varied grace." 1 Peter 4:10

MATH MAKES ME CRY

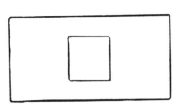

I have a love/hate relationship with numbers. I hate math and all of its formulas. Please don't make me find out what X is! I can do enough math to balance my checkbook (mostly), follow a recipe, and count crochet stitches. That's about it. But I love it when the numbers all add up; it gives me a nice righteous glow.

I had to take a calculus course when I was chasing my bachelor's degree. Keep in mind that this was **distance learning**, meaning that my college was actually in Birmingham, Alabama, a place where I have never been. The way it worked was they would send me a study guide with the required lessons, the name of the book I had to buy, and the name of my instructor.

So I am struggling through this calculus class, and it is taking me twice as long as the study guide says it should. It wasn't pretty, but I was getting it done. Until I came to this problem about a rectangle. You know...those things that have two long sides and two short sides? So

I follow the formula, which takes three pieces of notebook paper, and I get a square. You know, that thing that has four equal sides? Okay, fine. Calculus--1; Brogan--0. Even I can do that math.

Back to the notebook paper, pencil, and calculator and I get another square. Double check, triple check, redo. I fought with this freaking problem for three days and was sitting at the table bawling about it one night when Captain came home from chores and made the mistake of asking what's wrong.

What's wrong?! You want to know what's wrong? I'll tell you what's wrong. Math is stupid. Calculus is more stupid. I'm stupid. Cry, cry, swear, swear, throw the notebook across the room. Poor Captain...and then he made it worse.

He sort of chuckles and says, "A square can be a rectangle, but a rectangle can't be a square." What the fudge, you say? Sure enough, I looked in the glossary of the calculus book, and he was right. Damn him. Turns out Captain liked math in school and actually paid attention. Whoda thunk it?

Anyway, we'll rewind a little bit back to my first stint in college right out of high school chasing a two-year degree in business management. Mostly I just wanted to get the heck done with college so I could get married because Captain laid down the law there would be no wedding without a college degree. He is so harsh.

One of the required courses was accounting. I don't categorize accounting as math because accounting makes sense. The inflows have to equal the outflows to make a balance sheet. It's a puzzle, and I do love me a good puzzle. For the record, I **aced** accounting and all the rest of the courses, got my degree, and got the guy.

Fast forward 18 years, and we flounder into our own farming operation after Captain's dad retired. Now there is accounting right, left, and sideways, and it is up to me to keep track of it. Crap.

Part of the deal when we got our funding from Farm Service Agency was that we have to use a certain accounting software program through

Riverland College and the Farm Business Management program, and someone from that program has to come out a couple of times a year to check things over, do financial statements, blah, blah, blah. That means "the books" have to be up-to-date when the instructors calls and says he is coming. This usually catches me in a bad spot because, even though every stinking year I tell myself I am going to keep up with the books and enter the numbers every month when the bank statements come...I never do.

Why, you might ask? Let me tell you. From November 1 to March 1 in farming operation, it's nothing but stinking numbers. There are tax prep appointments to find out if we should prepay some accounts to offset a tax hit, year-end financial statements so the bank can decide if they are going to fund us for another year, cash flows so everyone involved knows if it was a good year or a bad year, and then there is the dreaded tax appointment in early February to have taxes filed by March 1. That's right. Agriculture income taxes have to be filed and paid by March 1, not April 15.

By the time all of that is over, I am so sick of numbers I ignore it all until about June. Then I have to go back to January 1 and try to remember what each check was for and if it is farm-related or personal. The statements from each vendor have to balance each month. The bank statements have to balance each month. Pass the Advil, I have a headache. Or I am bawling, much like the square and rectangle episode.

It really isn't even so much the **doing**, it's the *thought* of having to do. There are always so many better things I can do to occupy myself. However, once I get past the pain of starting, it goes fairly quickly and easily. I just need a kick in the butt to get started.

"And let us not grow weary of doing good, for in due season we will reap, if we do not give up." Galatians 6:9

HAPPY BIRTHDAY, BIG BROTHER

It is my big brother's birthday today! While he and I are sort of on the opposite ends of the spectrum--he's the science/math guy, and I am the reading/writing chick--we click pretty good. He isn't a big talker like his baby sister is, but when he says something, it is usually a pretty good idea to pay attention. I remember when I was getting ready to start kindergarten, he told me something I have never forgotten: You can never have too many friends. Wise even at 9 years old.

I think maybe that was the same year I sort of ruined his birthday party because Mom ended up taking me to the ER for an infected fingernail that needed to be incised and drained. Sorry about that, dude.

Big Brother is a wizard with a welder. He even competed at the state level in the high school VICA club...that would be the Industrial Arts Club. All things mechanical are in his wheelhouse. I remember when he took an old bicycle and modified it so that the seat was actually about six feet off the ground. Pretty cool stuff!

After high school, he spent four years in the Army serving our country as a tank mechanic and then used the benefits of the GI bill to get a degree in computer...things. I'm not exactly sure what he does, but it is WAY over my pay grade. He is one of the smartest people I know, but not all snarky about it.

When Princess went to college and had an apartment in the Cities, I didn't worry nearly as much as I might have because Big Brother and his family lived just two blocks away. She had to call upon him once or twice for mechanical issues with her car or computer stuff, and he helped out without complaint.

He married later in life, but when he picked The One, he nailed it. When they got married, he became a step-dad, and it thrills me at how well he took to that. Then again, I remember him having a ball playing with Young Man in the sandbox back in the day, too.

He was KISS, AC/DC, and Pink Floyd in high school compared to my George Strait, Reba McIntire, and Willie Nelson but over the years the differences have blurred, and now we are just siblings who love each other!

Happy Birthday and all my love always, Big Brother!

"A friend loves at all times, and a brother is born for adversity."
Proverbs 17:17

DATE NIGHT AND GROCERIES

Captain and I had date night last night...pizza and grocery shopping. Do we know how to live large or what? Actually, that is pretty traditional for us, and it works in our world. Mr. Pizza North is the place to go for a good pie in Rochester, Minnesota. Last night was the Big Peppi (double pepperoni) but usually we get Sharon's Favorite. I don't know who Sharon is, but she has good taste!

Rarely do we go for burgers. Captain's theory is that we have the best beef around in our freezer at home, so why pay for a burger. True statement; however, sometimes it is really nice to have someone ELSE cook the burger and bring it to me. He did finally concede that if he had to have burgers, Newt's was the place to go.

Then it was on to Hy-Vee North on 37th Street. We love Hy-Vee because when they say there is a helpful smile in every aisle...they aren't kidding. Grocery shopping for the last six months or so has been something of an adventure due to major remodeling there. I have had a spreadsheet on the computer for years with our most-often-purchased items listed in the order they are in the store. This eliminates the back-and-forth searching that happens if I just write a list freehand. Now that the remodeling is done, I find that my spreadsheet is all wrong. I mentioned to Captain last night that I should stop at the service counter and ask for a layout of the store with what is in which aisle. He advised waiting until the new Hy-Vee on 41st street opens up this fall, since we will shop there as it is 15 minutes closer. Good thinking, Captain!

I was banned from all things grocery for years because I either spent too much money or I bought the "wrong" stuff. Okay, fine, I bought fake cheese slices that wouldn't even melt for grilled cheese sandwiches...I have to have it held against me for a decade?! Buying groceries is shopping, and I hate shopping. Please don't make me do it. Captain is a shopper, at least at the grocery store. I don't care which price-per-unit is best, just put the damn stuff in the cart and let's get the hell out of here. And sometimes the cheapest product is not the best product. So there.

However, now I have been promoted to cart pusher and check writer. I occasionally may get to state an opinion, but rarely do I get to make decisions. Grocery stores just rattle me for some reason. Maybe it is all the choices available.

Take bread, for instance. Due to a recent diagnosis of prediabetes, I am now watching my carbohydrate intake. Obviously, the answer is to choose wheat bread over white bread. The problem there is I don't like the taste or texture of wheat bread. I don't care how much honey they put in it, it still tastes like plywood.

Picture the scene: local grocery store, crowded on a Sunday mid-morning, bakery section. I am looking at all the choices for non-white bread. I find a nice looking loaf of 9-grain that I could maybe tolerate. Woo and two hoos—it is made with wheat flour, so this is a good start. I am reading the nutrition label and get completely confused. Math is not my strong suit, but when the nutrition label says *serving size: ½ loaf* and *servings per container: 12*, even I know that math is wrong. I called Captain back from the cheese case to commiserate with me about this. Apparently I was a little abrasive about my confusion because he threw his hands up and walked away like he didn't know me. Fine, I'll try the regular bread aisle instead.

Have you been in the bread aisle lately? There are more varieties to choose from than Dolly Parton has wigs. How is anyone supposed to settle on one? Captain came to me with a loaf labeled Brown Bread. Very dense, made with wheat flour, low carbs. Okay, worth a try. Meanwhile, I have to walk past the Wonder Bread drooling since that would have been my first choice.

Since Captain is also supposed to be watching his diet by cutting down on the cholesterol, I headed for the freezer section to get some perch fillets. Again, I found unlimited choices of walleye, mahi-mahi, tilapia, cod, and haddock, but not one single perch fillet. We settled for tuna in a can but not until after the packed-in-water or packed-in-oil debate.

I could go on and on because I haven't even touched on the dairy case or the chip aisle. At any rate, I am pretty sure the management staff on site was glad to see us leave. Those helpful smiles were slipping a little bit by the time we checked out. Although we did make the cashier smile over our "guess the total amount" game. I rarely win this game because it involves math, but twice in the last two months, I nailed it. Once, I was within **pennies** of the final amount. Yay me!

Sometimes choices are good, but when the choices are so overwhelming as to be impossible...go for the chocolate!

"Go, eat your bread with joy, and drink your wine with a merry heart." Ecclesiastes 9:7a

NEVER FORGOTTEN

When our beloved dog died during the night when Young Man wasn't very old, it was the first time he had to deal with the life cycle ending. So we had a service, minus the eulogy and singing, complete with flowers and a grave marker. It made Young Man feel better to have had the service.

It made Captain and me rather reflective. We started talking about funerals in general, and then moved on to speculating on our own. Captain said he did not want anyone crying at his wake. He said he was going to rewrite his will to include specific instructions that, after the viewing of his body, everyone is to gather at our house to eat, drink, and be merry. He always loved a good party; that would be the Irish in him coming out.

Me, I want my wake to be a warm reminiscing of the person I was. I want Captain to tell about the time I hooked the bumper of his pickup on the guide wire of the yard pole and hyperventilated when I almost brought it crashing down on top of me.

I want Young Man to tell about the time I dressed up as Twinkle the Elf on Halloween and went trick-or-treating with him.

I want Princess to talk about the girls' weekend we had in Chicago with Captain's mom (some things were just too funny to stay in Chicago!).

I want my brothers to tell how we used to put Alka-Seltzer in our mouths and see who could keep their mouth shut the longest without foam pouring out.

I want my good friend to tell about the time we almost got asked to leave a kitchen gadget store one time for getting the giggles over something and causing something of a scene.

I want my FFA Parli Pro kids to talk about how Sargent Mom was tough but fair and just as surprised as they were when we advanced to state competition.

I don't know what stories Cubby and other grandchildren could tell because we haven't made those memories yet...but we will. Oh yes, you bet we will. Maybe it will be Gramma jumping in mud puddles with them. Maybe it will be Gramma reading a special book each and every time they stayed overnight. Who knows...but I hope they talk about it.

In the years since the dog was buried, our family has dealt with several tragic losses that have affected how Young Man and Princess view life. They have learned that when tragedy happens, family steps up and takes care of its own, friends come out of the woodwork with support and love, and God takes you through each minute, hour, day, and week that passes until you find your "new normal." I think they have gained a better understanding of "love your neighbor" through these losses, but I wish they had not had to learn it this way; the burial of our family dog was more in line with how I wanted them to learn this.

One of those losses was my dad in 2003. I don't think about him every day like I used to, or even every week. But on those special days...his birthday, Father's Day, Christmas, and Groundhog's Day (his favorite holiday)...he comes to mind clear as day. I still cry when those thoughts come, but all that tells me is that he was special, and he isn't forgotten.

I once saw a plaque that said, "When a loved one becomes a memory, the memory becomes a treasure." I wouldn't mind being treasured, but mostly I just want to be remembered. Not necessarily in grand fashion or with awe. Just as a person who did the best she could most of the time and the worst she could when she got in that kind of mood. To know that hopefully someone, somewhere, was positively affected by my having been on this earth. To know that I left a legacy of love, laughter, and friendship to those I leave behind.

"The Lord is near to the brokenhearted and saves the crushed in spirit." Psalm 34:18

CLASS DISTINCTIONS...I MEAN REUNIONS

I hated high school. No, that actually isn't an accurate statement. I hated the way I felt about myself in high school--inadequate and inconsequential. Some of that is on me, but some of it is on a large percentage of my classmates.

In high school, I wasn't pretty, I wasn't smart, and I wasn't athletic. I was a socially awkward poor farm kid in a school full of kids whose parents were doctors and IBMers. I was a have-not in a school of haves. I wasn't bullied so much as I was ignored. I didn't even blip on the radar of the cool kids, but if I did blip for them, I became a target of condescension or ridicule.

I'm not saying I don't have fond memories of my high school years. I had a core group of very good friends, and we had a lot of good times together. But, we were half a dozen in a class of almost 500, so it was easy for the haves to just not see us--me--on a daily basis.

Captain went to a smaller, rural school where it just wasn't possible to be ignored. In his class of under 100 kids, he knew everybody and everybody knew him. When we were flipping through our yearbooks once long ago, he could tell me at least one tidbit of information about not only every kid in his class, but just about every kid in the yearbook.

On that background comes the story. We graduated high school 30 years ago now, which means there were class reunions. I have never once been to one of my reunions for a variety of reasons. In the first few go-rounds, we couldn't afford it (remember, I went to the school of haves). On top of that, my core group of friends got together as a group once or twice a year anyway. But the crux of it was, I didn't like 95% of my classmates in high school so why would I pay good money to mingle with people I never liked and had nothing in common with?

This year, Captain encouraged me to finally go. He was working that night, so I went by myself only because I knew that some of my good friends would be there. After 30 years, you'd think we would all be on an even playing field. We have all gotten older, gained a little weight or lost a little hair, have had good things happen, and have had bad things happen. Apparently the lines of cool and not cool never blur because, of the 60 classmates there, no one mingled outside of their clique. The cheerleaders sat at one table, the jocks were at another table, and the yuppies were at yet another table. Then there was the table of me and my friends.

Again, some of that is on me because, while none of the other groups made an effort to mingle with me, neither did I make any kind of effort to mingle with them. It was a self-defense mechanism because I just didn't want to take the chance of being ignored again or made to feel any of the things I felt in high school. That's sad. I'm sure there are some very nice people in those other groups. Not everyone hangs on to the...identity, I guess...that they had in high school. Still...making the effort wasn't worth the chance that they hadn't changed.

In contrast, a month after my reunion, we went to Captain's 30-year reunion, and we had a blast. It was a smaller group--less than 30 people--but everyone talked with everyone, and not just the small talk kind of thing. Classmates sat down together, exchanged stories about work, spouses, and children. There were even two people there who went to school with Captain for a lot of years but had moved away and actually graduated from different high schools. Seriously, how wonderfully inclusive is that? That says "You were important to us."

At one point while Captain was off with classmates swapping stories, I sat with the spouses at a table, and we had the nicest conversation even though we only ever see each other every five years.

I have always enjoyed Captain's reunions for the simple fact that these people--who didn't know me back when--have always, without fail, made me feel welcome. Always.

Part of that may be because I have been part of this community now for 27 years, but I think it's more than that. I think a lot of it was because they grew up in a small community where status didn't mean as much as it did in the large urban school where I graduated. Maybe I still would have been something of an outsider if I'd been Captain's classmate, but I don't think so. I do know I wouldn't have been ignored.

I am at a stage of my life when I've gotten past what a friend of Captain's calls "the brain dead genius years" of young adulthood when everything is black or white with no gray areas. I have found that the bottom line is that I don't care about a person's race, color, religious preference, gender, sexual orientation, or political affiliation. If someone is nice to me, I will be nice to them. That's it. It really is that simple.

So here's to the PIHS class of '85. Thank you for welcoming me from the beginning and making me one of your own. K/A, folks.

"Gracious words are like a honeycomb, sweetness to the soul and health to the body." Proverbs 16:24

I DID THE BEST I COULD WITH WHAT I HAD

We watched Cubby for the afternoon on Sunday because Young Man and Mama Bear were having an outing with some friends. Got me some awesome Cubby time! She is so stinking cute, and just at that age where everything she does is adorable.

Like spilling water on the floor out of her sippy cup. Young Man and Mama Bear had come to pick her up, and we were all sitting in the living room visiting. Cubby was drinking out of her sippy cup, until she got bored with it and turned it upside down so the water dripped out onto the floor.

Like any good Nana, I just smiled at her and wiped up the mess. Young Man snarked about how HE would never have gotten away with that when HE was a kid. Dude, you were not as persecuted as you think you were.

But then I got to thinking before I fell asleep about how confusing it must have been to be a child of mine. Consider the variety of things I actually do remember saying to my children, often over the course of a single evening:

Don't run through the house!
Will you hurry up?
Speak up!
There is no need to shout at me.
I only have two hands, I can't do everything at once.
Pick up your clothes, put the toys away, and feed the cat.
I don't care who made the mess, I'm asking you to clean it up.
You spilled the milk all by yourself, you clean it up all by yourself.
Don't whine.
Fine, sit there and have a fit.
Good night, sweetheart. I love you too.

I also remember I used to lay in bed and pray for the knowledge, patience, and will to do better with my kids as the years went by.

Now I lay me down to rest, head on my pillow I lay.
I let my mind wander and drift over events that happened today.
I resurrect mistakes I made and march them through my mind.
And once again I make a vow to try to be more kind.
I think of my two children, fast asleep amid their dreams.
And think of how I hollered that their rooms are never clean.
Is cleanliness of such import that I could scarcely keep in mind
To show my children how to be gentle and how to be kind?
What lessons will they take when at last they leave our home?
Will criticism or love be the examples they have been shown?
When at last I stand on judgment day, before the Father of us all
Will I be granted my angel wings or will I make a fall?
Lord, please remind me that what all children need the most
Is love and respect and guidance, and to be cuddled, oh so close.
Now I lay me down to rest, with my head on my pillow I sleep.
This vow I make to you, oh Lord, please help me try to keep.

I don't know that I actually ever did a better job of it as time went on, but both of our children turned into upstanding, law-abiding, productive citizens. They both have gainful employment that they like and do well. They have people in their lives that they love. And they come home to see Mama once in a while, so I must have done something right. And it is my private joy that someday...not too far off...they'll be saying that prayer while they are lying in bed at night.

"Her children rise up and call her blessed; her husband also, and he praises her." Proverbs 31:28

MIDDLE CHILDREN...UNITE

August 12 has been designated by someone--and I would like to know who--as National Middle Child Day.

Then again, there is a "day" for everything. Seriously, I bet if you looked really hard you could find a National Eat Your Boogers Day because you know somewhere there are people who do that ***and like it***.

I get the reason behind Mother's Day (duh), Father's Day, and Grandparent's Day. Valentine's Day is just a hyped up holiday to sell candy and cards. What I want to know is what's the deal with Groundhog's Day?

Seriously people, spring will come when God decides spring is going to come and no vermin-infested rodent from some town that no one can pronounce in Pennsylvania will change that. And how does this stupid fur ball know that he **must** poke his head out of his hole on

February 2 in time to be seen live on the Today Show? Does someone call him and let him know? Does he have a little rodent alarm clock set to atomic time? What if he is a middle child groundhog and just doesn't want to conform?

As I look forward at other celebratory days on the handy little calendar I found online (yes, it was on the Internet, so it MUST be true) I see that August 27 is National Just Because Day. Seriously? We need to designate a day dedicated to doing something "just because"? Isn't that called spontaneity? Well, at least now you know if you see someone (or do something yourself) that might ordinarily be considered odd...you can play the "It's National Just Because Day" card. Go for it, let me know how that works for ya.

But back to today's celebration. Maybe middle children needed their own day because they have been maligned as trouble makers for years. I resent that, being a middle child myself. Why stereotype middle children, or anyone else for that matter. Who decides that firstborns are responsible, mature, and tend toward overachiever status? Who decides that last-borns are spoiled ingrates who got everything handed to them? And who in blue blazes thought it was a nice thing to label middle children as trouble makers?

I don't know what personality quirks other "middles" might have, but mine is procrastination. I put everything off and not just the big stuff like the farm books and the bills, it's the little stuff too. Take mailing a birthday card, f'rinstance. This is a four-day ordeal for me. Day 1--write out the card. Day 2--address the envelope. Day 3--put a stamp on the envelope. Day 4--put it in the mailbox. Seriously...what the fudge? I don't normally eat a big bowl of stupid for breakfast, so why is it so hard for me to accomplish a simple task like putting a birthday card in the mail?! I don't know. It's a study for the ages.

Salon appointments used to be the same way. I'd think to myself, *I need to get my hair cut.* And days--weeks--would go by until I would wake up one morning looking like Aunt Hilda Touched A Light Socket. At that point, there were no appointments available when I would call because--hey--all the smart people had called last week! I have figured this one out after years of Aunt Hilda episodes, and I make my next appointment before I leave the salon. So I'm a slow learner...flog me.

Maybe you don't have a celebration day, and maybe you do. I'll just say make every day a "Happy Day"...whatever day it is. Do things you like, see people you love, sing songs that make you happy. Have a happy!

"Bring the fattened calf and kill it. Let's have a feast and celebrate."
Luke 15:23

COMFORT ZONES

We all like our routines, me as much as anyone else. Sometimes it is good to try new things. Sometimes...not so much.

We like refrigerator pickles around here. I have always used the easy recipe from a Betty Crocker cookbook that I gave Captain for Christmas a few years ago. It's a good recipe but it has all this extra crap in it like carrots and onions. We just like salt and vinegar.

A little...and I do mean little...research on the Internet and I found a salt and vinegar fridge pickle recipe on a blog. Sounded easy enough and I had all the ingredients, so I put some together last week.

Remember how I said math wasn't my thing? Well, science really isn't either...they are both too logical for me. This is probably why I didn't realize that 3 teaspoons of pickling salt added to ½ cup of vinegar would be a nasty combination. That's all there was in each jar...sliced pickles, salt, vinegar, and some fresh dill...shake it up and put it in the fridge.

The blog I looked at said they were edible in an hour, so I tried one at supper. Holy pucker up, Batman! Drinking straight vinegar out of the bottle would have been better. Shake the three bottles up again, put them in the fridge on their lids, leave them overnight.

Nope, they weren't any better the next morning due to salt load. Captain might like them...he's a saltaholic...but I thought they were nasty. Like I said, science isn't my thing, but I did an experiment anyway. One jar I left alone. One jar I added half a cup of water and a teaspoon of sugar. The last jar I just added water to the top of the jar. Shook them all up again, turned them on their lids, and let them sit for seven days. I'm here to tell you that was an experiment that failed. They were still nasty, so it will be back to the Betty Crocker recipe.

Easy Refrigerator Pickles
6 cups thinly sliced unpeeled cucumbers
2 small onions, sliced
1 medium carrot, thinly sliced
1-¾ cup sugar
1 cup white or cider vinegar
2 tablespoons salt
1 tablespoon chopped fresh or 1 tsp dried dill weed

In a 2-½ to 3 quart glass or Tupperware container, layer cucumbers, onions, and carrot. In a medium bowl, stir remaining ingredients until sugar is dissolved; pour over cucumbers. Cover and refrigerate at least 24 hours.

I tried a new canned dill pickle recipe last year, but a different outcome. For a few years, I used Mrs. Wages pickling mix and then switched to the Ball Canning recipe. Mrs. Wages was pretty stout, and the Ball recipe was just okay. Back to the Internet. Found a canned dill pickle recipe with just salt and vinegar, and of course dill. No sugar, no spices. I was sure they were going to be awful, but they were AMAZING!

We finally had enough cucumbers from the garden a few days ago that I could make a batch of pickles. It was only three quarts, but it's a start. The recipe is so simple! I don't think I'm infringing on copyrights or revealing secrets since I found the recipe easily enough with a basic Google search.

Blue Ribbon Dill Pickles
8-½ cups of water
2-¼ cups white vinegar
½ cup pickling salt

Bring to a boil, remove from heat (or keep on **very** low simmer).

While all of that is going on, I have been running the jars and rims through the hottest, longest cycle on the dishwasher, and I am prepping the cucumbers. Just scrub them under cold water to remove those pricky things, slice a little bit off each end, and then line them up according to size. Anything smaller than my thumb I leave whole, but the rest I cut into spears.

Once the jars are done, I put a few sprigs of fresh dill in the bottom of each jar, pack in the cucumbers, and put another few sprigs of dill on top. Add the brine to each jar to ½ inch head space, removing any air bubbles from the sides of the jar with a butter knife or one of those fancy-schmancy air bubble removers. Place lids on and finger-tighten rims. Don't overtighten them.

My monster canner will hold seven quart jars, but if I don't have that many to process, I put empty jars filled with hot water in the canner as well, just to keep the filled jars from rattling around and breaking. Fill the canner with hot water to just below the jar necks. Cover and bring to **almost** a boil. Remove jars from the canner to a large bath towel. Cover the jars with the rest of the towel to cool and seal. Check lids for seal in 24 hours...but they will probably ping before that. LOVE that ping!! Once the jars have sealed, write the date on the lid with a Sharpie, because pickles need to cure for six weeks for optimum taste. Longest six weeks of my life...

We have enough harvested from the garden again to make another batch. We are also overrun with zucchini because Captain's mom is the only one who eats them, and she has been on vacation in Spokane for three weeks. The steers like them, though, so that is good.

We are anxiously awaiting the tomato harvest because we are completely out of pizza sauce, pasta sauce, salsa, and vegetable soup and nearly out of chili base. Not cool! I used Mrs. Wages for the pizza, pasta, and chili products but I do a homemade salsa. Hopefully I get the two weeks of vacation I asked for and the tomatoes are ripe at that time or else I am going to be crazy busy canning in the evenings and on weekends!

Just because things don't always work out the way we want or think they should, it is worth it to try something new once in a while because you never know when you will hit a gold mine. And if you hit big scoops of poop, you can always go back to the old way!

"He who gathers in summer is a prudent son." Proverbs 10:5a

MOTHER OF THE GROOM TALES

Trying to uphold society's perception of "the perfect image" as a middle aged woman holds a lengthy list of challenges. Besides the whole wrinkle thing (which, if you are smart, you will refer to as badges of honor), there is the fact that at a certain point, Newton's law of gravity takes over and you end up with furniture disease—your chest is in your drawers.

Men, you can take a break here and go get a beer; the following discussion will be lost on you because all YOU have to do to look dashing at an event is comb your hair and put on some nice cologne.

Women, grab the chocolate and a glass of wine and let's settle in for a chat.

Young Man got married several years ago to a lovely young lady. While we all know that everyone's eyes are on the bride on her wedding day, as the mother of the groom I knew there were going to be eyes on me as well.

Wouldn't you think that the best place to find a mother of the groom dress would be at a wedding store? Take my advice and skip this step. Your choices will either be Matron of the Year or mom-turned-tramp. There was nothing in between. The dresses were either floor-length with high necks and long sleeves or something with less fabric in it than my average dish towel. Seriously?!

Fine; we will move on to the higher end clothing stores and see what's what. Better choices but ungodly prices. Okay, we'll wait and hit the high end stores at clearance sale time.

My fashion guru is Princess (who looks elegant in tinfoil, mind you) and my mother-in-law, so off we went to an outlet mall near Princess's apartment. We hit pay dirt in the second store and found a very nice dress that would do quite well for the wedding, plus wasn't so fussy that it wouldn't also work for future dressy affairs I might need to attend.

Problem? It was fairly tailored and showed all of my Villages of Cellulite and Subdivisions of Fat that I have learned to disguise with strategic clothing choices over the years. So it was on to the foundation garment section of a local department store.

Have you been in one of these sections recently? There are thousands of choices for bustiers, girdles, booty-shapers, body shapers, and thigh shapers all designed by some evil, sadistic little elf with nothing better to do than imagine a Shamu-sized woman trying to fit into an Ariel-the-mermaid-sized article of clothing.

What I discovered after locking myself in the dressing room with a dozen different devices of torture was that while no matter which piece I put on to shape some body part…it just squeezed and bulged out in other places. It was like trying to hold raw egg in your hand. Got the thighs sort of under control where the shaper thing was…but beneath and above the shaper…bulges that were worse than what I started with. Belly flattener/shaper—yeah, that gave me panty lines the size of the Grand Canyon.

After many tears and words I would slap my children for, I found the least crappy looking thing and bought it without consulting my fashion gurus. They were miffed, but I couldn't handle any comments at that point.

I had that shaper staring at me for several months while the wedding got closer and closer. Trust me, I could hear it snickering at me in my sleep, but I was determined not to embarrass Young Man and his bride on their big day by looking like a fancy sack of potatoes in the family pictures.

A crash exercise program and some creative calorie counting got me into the control top nylons, the evil torture device, and the dress for their wedding. Did I look like Jennifer Aniston…not even close (of course, I never did so what do you expect). However, I looked respectable enough that no one ran screaming in terror.

Will it matter in five or ten years what I looked like on their wedding day? Nope, not a bit. Will anyone even remember what I wore? Probably not. What matters is that I got to be there to celebrate with them as they asked God's blessing as they started their new life together.

"Charm is deceitful, and beauty is vain, but a woman who fears the Lord is to be praised." Proverbs 31:30

NAME THAT TUNE

Music moves us. It's a primal reaction for whatever reason. We all have "that" song that either makes us cry every single time or makes us laugh. Why is that and what are they?

I recently polled friends and family and got the gamut in return from old classic hymns like How Great Thou Art, Silent Night, and Amazing Grace to novelty songs like The Streak, Teddy Bear, Who Wears Short Shorts, and Little Yellow Polka Dot Bikini. Then there is The Wedding Song, Daddy Dance With Me, The House that Built Me, Daddy's Hands, Stars and Stripes, and Jesus Loves Me. Every song had a reason for the reaction, sometimes a milestone event like a wedding and sometimes a memory from childhood.

Music has been a part of the human experience since the beginning. Music has been used for praise, to tell stories, or to call men to war with drums, flutes, or bagpipes.

Young Man and Princess mock me because even now as a grandmother, I cannot sing Puff The Magic Dragon without crying. Well, I am sorry, but when the verse about dragons living forever but not little boys…what am I supposed to do? Even when it was part of my third grade class sing-a-long, I cried. I know it is supposed to be about marijuana, but to me it's about how sometimes even the most precious relationships end, and that's sad.

My "always makes me smile song" is Snoopy's Christmas. You just gotta love Snoopy, and then if you add the whole goodwill-toward-men thing from the Red Baron, well that's worth smiling about.

I have Snoopy on my iPod. I know, I know…iPods are out of date and I should get with the program and have music on my phone. I'm not that smart so I'll stick with the iPod, thank you very much! My iPod is also loaded with Lady Gaga, KISS, AC/DC, Merle Haggard, George Jones, and the Mormon Tabernacle choir. What can I say; I have eclectic taste in music. Mostly I have two parameters for a "good" song. It either has to make me want to chair dance (badly) or it chokes me up. Now that I am a Nana, I will be loading nursery rhymes so I can groove it out with Cubby, and nothing anybody says will make me regret it.

Captain doesn't particularly have favorite songs; although Young Man and Princess will always talk about their dad stomping around in the morning belting out "Bare Necessities" to wake them up. Captain is more into advertising jingles like the very, very old Sears Christmas jingle, the ever-popular Menards jingle, and the Armour hot dog jingle. These are what he will sing on a daily basis. Sometimes it will be songs from 4-H camp, like "Do Your Ears Hang Low" and "Honky the Donkey."

But, if you ask him specifically, he will say that Rodney Atkins' song "If You're Going Through Hell" is his theme song. It harks back to his family's motto of don't let anything stand in your way, and it's gotten him through some pretty rotten days I guess.

They say music soothes the savage beast. It helps us celebrate, grieve, amuse, and educate. Here's to only high notes in your lives.

"Is anyone among you suffering? Let him pray. Is anyone cheerful? Let him sing praise." James 5:13

LIFE SKILLS

I saw a post on Facebook last night about the *things* (they used a naughty word) that all young adults should know how to do like check the oil in a car, change a tire, balance a checkbook, drive a stick shift, cook something more than mac-n-cheese, and how to do basic first aid. The premise was that these skills should be taught in a classroom.

Our premise is that parents should step up there, although I sort of dropped the ball on most of those things. However, I did teach Princess how to balance her checkbook. Created a monster there because when I balance my personal checkbook--not the farm books--if I am within $20 of what the bank says I have, I'm good with that. Nope, she has to have it Down To The Penny.

Princess operates mostly on a debit card, and she has saved every single receipt she has ever gotten since she first got her debit card back in high school. That's about five years' worth of receipts! Good for her, I say. Not that I don't save my receipts because you just never know when you might have to return something or get audited by the IRS, but hers are in chronological order. That's just a little bit crazy.

My poor children do not know how to cook anything more than mac-n-cheese or maybe tacos. Not because I didn't cook to give them an example. No, it's because in my house, I don't like people in my kitchen when I am cooking. You can sit on the other side of the snack bar and keep me company, but don't get in my space please.

Captain, on the other hand, viewed meal preparation as a family event and **everybody** had to help. So if my kids know how to cook anything, it's due to Captain's influence, not mine.

Captain also taught the kids how to check the oil in their vehicles, same as my daddy taught me. My daddy also taught me how to change a tire by making me take off and put on all four tires when I got my first car while he stood by and watched.

That came in handy one day in college when I came out to find a flat tire on my car. Apparently someone had gone through the parking lot and let air out of tires because just as I got done putting on my spare, three other people came over and asked if I would change their tires as well. And, get this, two of them were GUYS! I made $50 that day changing tires. Thanks, Daddy!

The other thing that we drilled into our kids that they took to heart was the evils of credit cards. They saw us get upside down on credit card debt when they were young and learned how painful it is to restructure a budget to pay all that off. We all went without a lot of *things* (insert naughty word) during the four years it took to get that accomplished, so they are extremely aware of being responsible with their credit.

As far as first aid goes, in this house, first aid usually involves the emergency room unless it's just a shaving cut. Captain learned after two or three trips with something stuck in his eye (cornstalks, piece of metal) that the emergency room uses the Life, Limb, Vision triage method, and if you are in danger of serious damage to or loss of one of those things, you get bumped to the top of the list.

Young Man tended to be accident prone in his teenage years, so we spent many a-night in the emergency room with lacerations, contusions, broken bones, and an emergency appendectomy. Young Man's trips to the emergency room started when he was 2 years old and got into another daycare kid's bottle of Ventolin and chugged it like Kool-Aid. Yeah, he was TOP of the list in the ER that day due to near-death circumstances. Freaking scary times.

In comparison, Princess only had a couple of major events in the emergency room--one for getting teat dip (that's a chemical solution applied to cow udders to kill bacteria) in her eye and once for the rabies vaccination series after getting chomped on by a neighbor's dog with no vaccination papers. Even though they don't do the shots in the belly button for 12 days in a row anymore, it is still an extremely unpleasant experience! However, she did spend a night in the hospital at six weeks old with an unexplained fever. More freaking scary times. Yeesh!

While practical skills of vehicle, finance, and health maintenance are essential and should be part of every one's wheelhouse, I hope we also taught our kids the more abstract life skills of honesty, hard work, mutual respect, and perseverance, and that they will teach their kids those things as well.

"Train up a child in the way he should go; even when he is old he will not depart from it." Proverbs 22:6

LAUNDRY DAY

Laundry day (which is actually every day) at my house is like an archaeological dig. Sorting through the pile of dirty clothes can clearly show the events of recent days.

A pile of soggy towels used to tell of a water fight on a warm summer evening that got a little out of hand. Whereas everyone else was satisfied with glasses of water as missiles, Captain went for the "big guns" and filled a couple of 5-gallon pails to douse us with. Really, he should know better than that, because we paid him back in full when I distracted him with a couple of hugs and kisses while the kids hooked up the hose and turned it on.

Stacks of clean, folded shirts and pants in the dirty clothes hamper used to tell me that my children had "cleaned" their rooms recently. That must really be a kid's trick, because I remember doing the same thing. There was always something more important to do than clean—what, I can't imagine--but there must have been something.

A pile of children's bedding can bring back memories of a nerve-wracking night during a high fever episode. Any parent who has done that knows what crazy thoughts run through the mind at 3 a.m. I wonder if God gets a good laugh from all the ludicrous deals that are flung His way in times of such crises. In my book, God has to have a sense of humor or He wouldn't be able to tolerate the human race at all.

Ah yes, there was always the dreaded chore clothes layer. If Captain had an especially busy week, I might find grease, hydraulic oil, or blood...or a combination thereof...like the day after the tractor went kaput in the middle of the field when they were chopping hay. There might be shirts with a large blob of sour milk on it—that says, "teaching a calf to drink out of a pail" to me. It takes a few days of lessons for most of the milk to end up inside the calf rather than on the outside of Captain. I don't even ask what happened when clothes have various bovine body fluids all over them. Those are usually the nights he comes in the house especially cranky and talks about selling "all those dumb animals."

Back in the day when Princess folded laundry, we would go from archaeological dig to treasure hunt because not everyone's clothes ended up in the right dresser. I can understand how a sweatshirt or pair of jeans might look the same, but I really couldn't understand how my foundation garments ended up in Young Man's pile of clothes. Neither one of us was very happy with that mix up.

I take as many shortcuts on laundry day as I can. I don't mind washing and drying them because—hey—the machines do the work, right? I dislike folding them and putting them away. That's why I don't fold socks at all...everybody's socks go in a bucket and we do the grab-and-go thing. I'm actually preserving the life of the socks because the elastic doesn't get all stretched out by repeated folding. That's my story and I am sticking to it!

If anyone else were to do my laundry, there would be no significance at all in these layers of clothes, but since I view the laundry room as my meditation room (you can get a lot of thinking done while folding towels), I cherish the memories I find while excavating.

"Strength and dignity are her clothing, and she laughs at the time to come." Proverbs 31:25

CREEPY CRAWLIES

I don't consider myself to be a squeamish person...possible nocturnal campground encounters with Bigfoot notwithstanding. Most creepy crawly things don't bother me. Bats are okay as long as they are outside. If they came in my house, I might freak out, but I've never had to test that theory.

Same with snakes. I think they are interesting in their display cases at Oxbow Zoo, but if there was one coming at me in its natural habitat, I might freak out.

Spiders...well, it depends on what kind. The daddy longlegs that I find in the bathtub now and then are harmless. However, several years ago when we rented pasture land from a neighbor and had to walk the fence cutting down weeds--that would be a 5-strand barbed wire fence--we ran into some of those nasty black spiders with the yellow spots or stripe on the back. Yeah, everybody but Captain vaulted OVER the fence. I'd have gone right through the dang fence if I'd needed to. Eeeeeuuuwww!

Now mice, they don't bother me at all. I know a lot of women who jump on chairs and scream bloody murder at the sight of a mouse. My first reaction is *Well you little stinker, where did you come from?* And then I set out traps. The spring that Princess graduated high school, we had some mice in the house, so I set some snap traps. Those little critters were sneaky and would get the peanut butter (yes, this works better than cheese) off the trap and never trip the trap.

Undaunted, I set a series of traps along the wall beneath the picture window, behind the entertainment center, and behind the couch. No sneaky little rodent was going to get the best of me!

There I was watching TV one night, and Mr. Mouse comes scurrying at warp speed along the wall beneath the picture window. As I watch him approach the first trap, he skids to a screeching halt, stopping a whisker-breadth away from the trap. He takes a minute to observe the trap ahead, then beats a retreat to think about it.

Next thing I see is Mr. Mouse stealthily sneaking along the wall. He skirts around the first trap, narrowly avoids the second trap, and completely misses the third trap. What the fudge?! Now it's war.

I upgraded from the snap traps to the glue traps. I put the blob of peanut butter smack in the center of the trap and set them out. No way could Mr. Mouse get to the PB without stepping in the sticky part of the trap. And that stuff **sticks**, let me tell you! Ask Dipstick, who laid in one once and had it stuck to his side for about a week. Brogan--1; mouse--0.

Anyway, so creepy crawlies. The one thing that will make me lose my mind in terror is grasshoppers. When I was a kid, Dad grew oats that had to be stored in the grain bin. It was my job to get up in the gravity box and push all the oats down toward the door where they then went into the auger and finally into the grain bin. Oats are loaded with grasshoppers, and by the time I would finish emptying the wagon, I had grasshoppers in my hair, up my pants legs, and down my shirt. The boogie woogie bugle boy had nothing on me trying to dance those suckers out of my clothes.

So imagine my distress when I discovered a mutant, overgrown grasshopper clinging to the wall of my bedroom! No lie, this thing was at least six inches long. That's just wrong.

That thing was FREAKING gross! When I saw that, my heart almost stopped. Since I didn't have a bazooka handy, I got my trusty fly swatter (on sale at Menards, thank you very much). It took me 30 seconds to even get close enough to swing with the swatter because I didn't know if it was going to jump or fly at me, which would have just put me on the floor in a puddle of panic.

I finally screwed up my courage and took a swing. I killed it dead as Moses with the fly swatter, but then the dead carcass came flying off the wall right at me. I'm not too proud to admit I screamed like a little girl. It landed on the floor, so I threw a towel over it and stomped on it half a dozen times just to make sure it was really dead because you never know with those nasty, evil things. I ran out of the room whimpering and made Captain dispose of the body. Twenty-four hours later, I still had the willies.

As I read this over, I realize I need to revise my original statement to: Damn right I am squeamish about creepy crawly things!!

"All winged insects that go on all fours are detestable to you."
Leviticus 11:20

TAGLINES

If you ever think that advertising doesn't pay...think again, my friend. Some tag lines stick with you more than others and last generations. I tracked down some well-known tag lines and have left a blank where the product/brand name would be. Some of these were from before my time, and I still know them because my parents repeated them over and over and over. How many can you guess <u>without Googling them</u>? Answers will be given later. Good luck!

1. You're in good hands with _____
2. Flick my _____
3. _____take me away
4. _____--we bring good things to life
5. Please don't squeeze the _____
6. Cooks who know trust _____
7. Aren't you glad you use _____
8. Nothing sucks like _____
9. Don't get mad, get _____
10. Pardon me, do you have any _____
11. How about a nice _____

12. _____ puts you in the driver's seat
13. Pure clean, pure _____
14. Nothing runs like a _____
15. Every kiss begins with _____
16. Do the _____
17. _____ hits the spot
18. With a name like _____, it has to be good
19. I coulda had a _____
20. Bye-bye, buy _____

"Remember the former things of old." Isaiah 46:9a

THE TALE OF THREE FRANKS

Friday was a beautiful day for one last camping trip to Whitewater State Park. Because I had to work in the morning, Captain took care of the packing. At noon on the dang dot, I clocked out and we hit the road.

We were crossing our fingers for a first come/first served site being available, and luck was with us...we got the last one! We found the site and got everything set up. This is when we realized that, once again, we had forgotten the camp chairs. Oh well, the picnic table would just have to do for lounging.

Captain wanted to hike to Inspiration Point which is a bluff overlook area facing south from the state park. The first part of the trail was a couple of hundred stone steps. By the time we got to the top--with two breaks for me to catch my breath--I was done. A very nice lady asked me as I was wheezing and panting on the bench along the trail if I would like her to take my picture with my husband. Yep, I'm looking my best right now with beet-red cheeks and sweat running...well, everywhere...but okay.

We looked at the trail map, and Inspiration Point was about another ¾ mile and labeled "difficult." NO thank you! I gave Captain the camera and told him to have a good time. I'd just go back to the trailhead and wait for him. Off he went.

I traipsed back down the stairs, which for some reason seemed even worse than going up. I got to the bottom and realized I'd better keep moving or I was going to cramp up something fierce. As I was walking across the park area, I stopped at a kiosk with flyers posted on it about the park. Okay, I wasn't really reading the flyers, I was trying to look nonchalant while I panted my way back to regular breathing. I am an overweight, out-of-shape woman...sue me. But through the sweat running in my eyes, I saw an announcement for a nature program that night about an old cemetery in a nearby ghost town. Hmmmm...that sounded better than hiking!

I regained feeling in my legs and made it back to camp to wait for Captain. I told him about the cemetery thing, and since we both have an interest in old cemeteries, we decided to go. We had just enough time to make a quick supper first and clean up before we went to the Visitor's Center for the program.

The focus of the program was the town of Beaver, which was settled after the Civil War. The returning soldiers and their families found the fertile Whitewater River valley to be very good wheat-growing ground, so they cleared the flats to plant wheat but planted over the hills rather than across the hills (contour stripping), so erosion was a huge factor.

Unfortunately, they also cleared the hills of the trees to make grazing pastures for cows. After a few years of these practices, the flooding began because there was nothing to stop the heavy rains from washing down the steep hills and through the valley. In one particular year, Beaver flooded 28 times! The townspeople tried to recover year after year after year, but eventually nature won the battle and the town was abandoned.

It shouldn't technically be called a ghost town, because it is still there. It is just buried under 15 feet of sand, silt, and soil. It was the CCC that helped save the rest of the valley by replanting thousands upon thousands of trees on the bare hillsides and working to restore the wetlands in the valley.

Anyway, back to the story of Beaver. So, even though the town is gone, its cemetery is still there, maybe due to being at a higher elevation. It is beautifully maintained through a contract with the state park system. The naturalist who led the program had done an immense amount of research and told us something about half a dozen of the people buried there. One was the founding father of the town and a pillar of the community. His family planted a tree when he was buried...**160 years ago** that is still alive and thriving!

There is another spot that had a circle of cedar trees with two markers outside the circle and two markers inside. The markers inside the trees were for children that hadn't survived childhood, and the markers outside were for the parents.

There were two small markers in the middle where, the story goes, after a diphtheria outbreak in the town, a father had to go in the middle of the night by himself to bury his two young children because he didn't want to spread the virus to his friends and neighbors, so he had to grieve alone at the gravesides.

But the story that really caught me was the tale of the three Franks. Near the back of the cemetery was a row of markers for the Irish family (surname, not nationality). There was a girl whose name I can't remember, then a Frank, then another Frank, and then an Arvid. All children. The parents of these youngsters wanted a son named Frank, but had to bury two sons named Frank before the third one survived. Interesting stuff, but so darn sad!

I'm glad we went on that nature program, even though it was kind of sad. We learned things about a town in our own backyard that we hadn't even known existed. So the bucket list now has "attend a nature program at every state park" as well. It serves to remind me that the opportunities for education are everywhere if I just pay attention.

What? You act like you are waiting for something! Oh yes, I promised the answers to the tagline quiz! In the interest of full disclosure, I found these on the Internet and I only knew a handful of them off hand. Here you go!

You're in good hands with **Allstate**
Flick my **Bic**
Calgon take me away
GE--we bring good things to life
Please don't squeeze the **Charmin**
Cooks who know trust **Crisco**
Aren't you glad you use **Dial**
Nothing sucks like **Electrolux**
Don't get mad, get **Glad**
Pardon me, do you have any **Grey Poupon**
How about a nice **Hawaiian Punch**
Hertz puts you in the driver's seat
Pure clean, pure **Ivory**
Nothing runs like a **Deere**
Every kiss begins with **Kay**
Do the **Dew**
Pepsi Cola hits the spot (and as my dad used to say "ten minutes later hits the pot!")
With a name like **Smuckers**, it has to be good
I coulda had a **V-8**
Bye-bye, buy **bonds.**

Thanks for playing!

"This is what the Sovereign Lord says: On the day I cleanse you from your sins, I will resettle your towns, and the ruins will be rebuilt."
Ezekiel 26:33

DO IT YOURSELF DISASTERS

It is a commonly known fact that do-it-yourself home improvement projects drastically increase a couple's risk for divorce, but they don't hold a candle to farm chores done jointly by a husband and wife.

Take, for instance, chasing steers back into their yard after they've gotten out. I consider myself to be a reasonably intelligent person and, therefore, do not make it a habit to stand directly in the path of a 1500-pound moving animal; unless Captain tells me I have to if I ever want to get the steers back in the yard so we can go work on some home improvement project.

So I plant my feet wide apart, set my shoulders straight, and bravely face a thundering mass of horns and hooves. Okay, so there aren't really any horns, but there *could* be. When I succeed in keeping the steers from sneaking past me, my sense of accomplishment quickly evaporates in the deafening tirade from Captain that the steers, while not getting past me, still did not go in the yard because as luck, and his instructions, would have it, I WAS NOT IN THE RIGHT PLACE! By the time we got all the steers where they belonged, the only home improvement project on our minds was building separate bedrooms.

Silo unloaders are another good catalyst for farm divorces--ask any farm wife, and she will tell you the same thing. Silo unloaders have a tendency to break down, requiring someone (Captain) to climb the silo to see what is wrong and try to fix it. Because this usually takes several attempts in which the silo unloader needs to be started and stopped, another person (me) is required to stand at the bottom of silo running the power switch.

For those of you who don't know Captain, he has a very soft voice that doesn't usually carry across the kitchen table, much less down a 75-foot silo to where I am. Add to that disadvantage the fact that I am standing in the middle of 80 very hungry cows who are complaining at the top of their lungs. Captain can't quite understand that "yes" and "no" can sound very similar from inside a silo in this setting, causing confusion as to whether I am supposed to start the silo unloader or not. I once deciphered a message incorrectly and nearly took his finger off.

Perhaps the worst episode of silo unloader repair was the time Captain needed to adjust a doohickey attached to the thingamabob. Before he climbed up to check it out, he gave me my instructions. "Wait until I get up there and yell to turn it on. While it's running, don't worry that there isn't much feed coming down; I'll get it adjusted and yell for you to turn it off." Simple, right? WRONG!

He climbed the silo and yelled to turn it on. So far, so good. After I watched the silage trickle out of the chute for 20 minutes or so, it dawned on me there had to be a problem because I could hear a distinct banging on the silo chute. So, against direct orders, I shut the silo unloader off without his say-so. At that point, above the banging, I could hear muffled words filtering down the chute. Direct and immediate action seemed to be in order.

A little investigation on my part revealed the silo chute was plugged tight with silage. In a panic, I reached into the chute and began frantically digging out the silage. As I dug, the dialogue from inside the silo became more distinct, and I began to get a bad feeling. After 30 minutes of digging and hearing phrases that not only questioned my intelligence but cast doubt on my parentage as well, I almost quit digging to leave him in there, but I finally got the last of the silage out…and Captain.

When he asked what I thought I'd been doing and why hadn't I shut the silo off sooner, I reminded him (gently, mind you; I'm no fool) that he had said the silage would not be coming out fast. I won't go into his reply, but you can use your imagination to know what he said to me for plugging the silo chute with a good 20 feet of silage.

One story Captain likes to tell is about the time, on a bitterly cold day, he had to scale the roof to clean the wood stove chimney. I, of course, had to stand at the bottom of the ladder to make sure it didn't blow down while he was on the roof. When he finished, he found that the roof was too slippery to try and slide down to the ladder. So I told him to wait while I got a length of clothesline to use as a rescue rope. Disgust does not begin to cover how he viewed my offering of a 3-1/2 foot section of nearly-frayed clothesline. He actually suggested I might have an ulterior motive of trying to "do him in" for his life insurance. He has since learned that one does not insult the guard of the ladder or one ends up stranded on the roof on a bitterly cold day until such time as the guard of the ladder is sufficiently satisfied with the apology offered from the rooftop and puts the ladder back against the house.

I was, in time, forgiven for these incidents and have since experienced others. Through it all, Captain and I have managed to keep our marriage intact. Our buzz phrase now if such an episode occurs is "We married for better or worser…we just didn't know it would be this worser." It is our way of saying to each other, "I'm sorry" and "I forgive you." It is comforting to have such an informal way to apologize and be pardoned. Most of all, though, the phrase says, " I love you."

"So they are no longer two but one flesh. What therefore God has joined together, let not man separate." Matthew 19:6

IT'S A DOG'S LIFE

Hi, this is Dipstick writing today in honor of National Dog Day. Mrs. Captain is busy, so she handed the controls over to me.

For those of you who don't know me from having me chase your car when you drive by, I am an 8-year-old Lab/Dalmatian/Rottweiler. I don't know how Mr. and Mrs. Captain would get along without me, my mom, Dayzee, and my dad, Bear. We keep an eagle eye out for any suspicious activity. Excuse me while I chase a car...

Whew, got close enough that time to read the tire size! Where was I?

Oh yeah, our value to Mr. and Mrs. Captain. Well, first of all, we conduct daily soil borings to make sure that there are no seismic disruptions underground. The Captains don't seem to appreciate this at all, but it is absolutely necessary for us to dig large holes in various points of the yard to be thorough.

The Captains are also pretty harsh about our freedom of expression. Dogs have feelings too, and we need to talk about them. Okay, so fine, 3 a.m. might not be the ideal time for it, but what's a dog to do?

Excuse me, there is another car to chase.

Don't get me wrong, the Captains are good parents. We get our feeder filled every week, and every morning we get our doggie num-nums. Mom is such a suck up. SHE gets to go in the house for her num-num but me and Dad wait outside on the deck. The Captains try to make me shake for my treat, but after eight years they sort of gave up on that. Geez, just give me the goods and no one gets hurt!

Some farm dogs help chase cattle, but that's beneath me. I have much more important things...excuse me, another car going by.

I think cattle are dumb. What do they do...walk around, eat corn, drink water, and fart. I can do that too, but no one appreciates it.

Sometimes our cousin, Chewy, comes to visit but he is mostly a pain in the butt. Literally. He always has his nose in my business!

Another favorite activity of the Brogan Dogs is chasing bunnies. There are three of them around here. I tried that thing that Elmer Fudd talked about, but even being vewy, vewy, quiet doesn't help. Those little stinkers are gone in a flash.

We especially like it when the paper is delivered because the driver stops and gives us another treat. So does the FedEx man and the UPS driver. Too bad the Captains don't order much delivery stuff.

I was watching the TV through the living room window the other night and saw a commercial for The Cutest Pet contest and have been waiting for the Captains to come and take my picture, but the camera must be on the fritz because they haven't done it yet.

Oh how exciting, it's not a car this time but a guy on a bike...be right back.

Well, it's been nice catching up with you. I have to get back to my duties now.

"Whoever is righteous has regard for the life of his beast, but the mercy of the wicked is cruel." Proverbs 12:10

MINNESOTA STATE FAIR

My what a busy few days it has been! We had an overnight with Cubby on Friday, I had a girls' outing with Captain's mom and Princess on Saturday, and we did up the Great Minnesota Get Together with some good friends on Sunday.

Since Captain and I started dating 30 years ago, we have only missed one state fair, and I really can't even remember why. Must have been something major, though.

We have gone by ourselves some years, some years we just took the kids, and other years we have gone with friends. We always try to go on 4-H livestock weekend whether our kids were showing or not. Young Man had multiple trips with livestock, both with his dairy cow and with dairy steers. Princess had non-livestock exhibits two different years as well.

We have our favorite things to do every year, but the biggest must see is the butterheads being carved. If you tell me you don't know what the butterheads are, you are seriously lacking in your Minnesota history education!

Princess Kay of the Milky Way is the goodwill ambassador for Minnesota's dairy industry. The first Princess Kay was crowned in

1954, making it the second longest running dairy ambassador program in the country, second only to Wisconsin's Alice in Dairyland. And Alice doesn't get carved in butter like Princess Kay does.

Each year since 1965, Princess Kay and her 11 court attendants each spend a day in a revolving refrigerated glassed-in display area having their likeness carved from a 90-pound block of butter provided by AMPI out of New Ulm, Minnesota. For the last 40 years, sculptor Linda Christensen has churned (see what I did there?) out entertainment for millions of state fair goers.

We have known a few ladies who have had butterheads over the years, and we can even say we had a Princess Kay in our wedding, even though she completed her reign three weeks before we got married. I happened to find a picture of her butterhead being carved when we were going through the new State Fair History Center where Heritage Square used to be.

We love history around here because you never quite know everything about anything, and there is always something new to learn.

Other highlights for us are the 4-H building where the best of the best from 4-Hers across the state is displayed. Personal favorites for me are the photography exhibits and the woodworking exhibits. Plus, if we time our visit to the 4-H building right, we also get to see the 4-H Arts In performance.

Captain and our friends made it into the 4-H building while Princess and I were checking out some lawn swings outside the building. I was trying to get a picture of the Curious George mascot when suddenly, Captain comes back out the door like a bullet and insists, "I found something you just have to buy." Well, after I picked myself up off the ground where I'd fainted (Captain never makes impulse purchases...EVER), I followed him into the entryway where the Clover Store is. They sell clothing and accessories related to the promotion of 4-H. Oh. My. Gosh. There were the cutest little white onesies that said in bright green lettering, "I want to be a Minnesota 4-Her when I grow up!" He was right--we had to buy that!

The Horticulture Building houses FFA and open class exhibits and is home each year to Minnesota's Biggest Pumpkin which this year weighed in at a hefty 1473 pounds! We've got steers out here that weigh just about that much! Perusing the educational booths on various aspects of agriculture production in Minnesota is often entertaining, and this year Princess learned that Crystal Sugar is made from sugar beets, so she can no longer say that beets "taste like dirt."

As always, food was a big part of the state fair experience with the usual staples of cheese curds, Sweet Martha's cookies, Aussie potatoes, and poutine, but we always like to try one of the new foods they have. This year's choice was the maple bacon funnel cakes in the food building. Holy sugar high, batman....but oh so worth it!

We don't do rides as a rule, but this year Princess agreed to ride the space needle with Captain while our friends and I sat in the shade and rested while we waited for them. When the kids were younger, we couldn't leave the fairgrounds before riding Ye Old Mill. When we were in the History Center earlier, I saw a little tidbit that there have actually been weddings at Ye Old Mill for people who either fell in love or got engaged there in years past. Sweet!

One of our last stops is always the International Bazaar (or as we call it, the Bizarre Bazaar) because...WOW...there is some weird stuff in there! Best stop of the day is the stall that sells leather purses, and this year was no different. I don't care what anyone says...a woman can never have too many purses.

So our annual State Fair trip is over. It doesn't matter how many times we go, the adventure is always new and fun! If you've never been to the Great Minnesota Get Together...first of all, shame on you...and second, don't let another year go by without at least giving it a whirl one time.

Pass the cheese curds!

"My son, eat honey, for it is good, and the drippings of the honeycomb are sweet to your taste." Proverbs 24:13

HAPPY BIRTHDAY, CAPTAIN!

I am afraid that in my quest for humor, I might paint an incorrect picture of my relationship with Captain. It could appear by what may be written that I have little respect for this man who calls me Spouse. My birthday present to him today is this retraction/disclaimer because nothing could be further from the truth. Don't get me wrong, he will still have the starring role in many posts because--hey, he's the only readily available target--but always, always, always in good humor, respect, and love.

There is no finer man alive than the one I look at across the dining room table every night. Never once in the years of our courtship and marriage has a single birthday, Valentine's Day, or anniversary gone by without his sending or bringing me flowers to commemorate the day--sometimes hand-picked wild flowers. Those are the best! He may be the first to tease me about my lick-and-a-promise style of housekeeping, but he is also my staunchest motivator when I get down on myself. He tries not to fuss if…when…I make an impulsive purchase.

He was right by my side through two births, holding my hand and encouraging me to that moment when we first saw each of our two children. He never failed to kiss them goodnight and tuck them in. He was their buddy, and they loved to romp and play with him. The few times I ever scolded them for bothering Daddy when he was tired after a long day, he told me to let them be and let them play because they grow so quickly and will one day be too busy to play with dear old Dad.

I have seen him work long, dirty, back-breaking hours to provide us with food, shelter, and clothing. I have watched with pride as he received the second highest honor handed out by the National FFA organization. I have seen him accept recognition as well from a local civic organization for his accomplishments in agriculture.

I am eagerly looking forward to the day in the not too far future when Princess says she wants to marry someone just like her daddy. Then I can tell her that there is no other like her daddy. He is special, he is unique, and he was gracious enough to let me share his life. He is my husband, bless his soul, but above all else, he is my best friend.

Happiest of happy birthdays, Captain!

"As an apple tree among the trees of the forest, so is my beloved among the young men." Song of Solomon 2:3a

ATTITUDE OF GRATITUDE

Mama Bear reminded me today that in today's society, an attitude of gratitude is often missing.

So I got to thinking about what I am thankful for in my life.

I am always thankful when no one sees me slip on the ice. You know, those times when you do the whole windmill-your-arms and tap-dance-your-feet routines? When I'm lying there in the snow, I always think, *"Why didn't you just slip gracefully to the ground instead of making a damn production out of it?!"*

I am always glad at bowling league when my score has three digits in it. I really don't care which three digits...as long as I break 100, I am happy, happy, happy! This sometimes irritates Captain because, as the sponsor of our team, he would really like me to do better. Suck it up, Bunky; this is as good as it gets!

Speaking of bowling, I am always glad to have the chance to get together with the ladies and have a fun night of gossip and giggling.

I am always glad on those mornings I wake up and remember that I have nowhere to go, nobody to see, and nothing to do...which means I don't have to even <u>try</u> and look pretty. I can stay in my grunge clothes and pull my hair back into a scare-small-children messy bun.

I am always glad when I make it to the gas station, even if--or especially when--I am running on prayers and fumes.

I am thankful that artificial intelligence hasn't come far enough yet for my scale to yell at me when I step on it in the morning.

Then there are the big ticket items. The real things that I am thankful for every single day. My health, my job, my freedom.

But most of all I am so thankful every day for my family and friends who mean so very much to me.

"Oh give thanks to the Lord, for he is good, for his steadfast love endures forever!" Psalm 107:1

SLOANEY BALONEY

Labor Day 2007. It was as beautiful a fall day as you could ask for. Blue skies, light breeze, sunshine all around. Captain and I took the kids to Nelson, Wisconsin, to meet up with my mom and Baby Brother and his family. Just a laid back lazy day.

After brunch at the local restaurant, we drove down to Alma, Wisconsin, to the lock and dam to watch the river traffic. The kids all played tag around a wooden kiosk sign telling the history of the lock and dam there. The adults lounged on the grass in the shade and caught up on each other's lives.

It was one of those day that I will never, ever forget. Not one detail. Because it was the last day I ever saw my niece, Sloane. I took a picture of her that day, and it remains my favorite photo that I have ever taken.

Sloaney Baloney, as she was called by her family, was sort of a surprise to Baby Brother and his wife. They had already adopted a beautiful daughter two years earlier and never expected to be pregnant, but God had other ideas. She blessed their lives for 15 short months before God wanted her back and took her home to Him.

My brother's family's strongest wish is that Sloane be remembered. For this reason, they set up an endowment fund in their local community in Sloane's name to help children as a tribute to their daughter. Turning their sorrow into something positive for others makes me so humbled, because I don't know if I would be that selfless in the same situation.

There is nothing that eases the grief of a parent who has lost a child-- not one damn thing. I wish there was so I could do that for my brother and his wife. All I can do is let them know that I love them and I will always remember Sloane running around with her sister and cousin's on a beautiful, breezy Labor Day by the river.

"Blessed are those who mourn, for they shall be comforted."
Matthew 5:4

DIRT DON'T HURT

Tomato canning season is upon us again, and not a moment too soon! We are out of pizza sauce, pasta sauce, chili base, and salsa.

I didn't come to the canning and preserving game until just a few years ago. Don't ask me why. Now that I have, it is one of those things where I can hardly contain my excitement at the beginning and by the end I am cursing every jar, every lid, every tomato. But then, when I crack the seal on one of the jars to make a good home-cooked meal over the winter, I am back to excited and satisfied.

So the first order of business this year is the pizza sauce. Captain is a pizza fiend, and not the frozen pizza from the grocery store, either. He makes it from scratch. Well, sort of scratch.

He used to buy the pizza dough mix and roll it out himself, and I have tried this as well, and neither one of us is any good at it. It finally got to the point where we just decided to buy the ready-made pizza crusts and call it good. However, the sauce is homemade and the burger is home grown, so I call that "from scratch."

Anyway, I had enough tomatoes recently to do a batch of pizza sauce. I remember the old days when you had to blanch the tomatoes, ice-bath them, then core and peel them. In today's modern world, however, that process was greatly reduced when I bought a Sauce Master. No more blanching, coring, and peeling. Just quarter the tomatoes, skin and all, and run them through the SM. There are different sized screens to use for however chunky you want it. For pizza sauce, I use the smallest screen made so it basically makes a puree.

After that, it is just a matter of adding the Mrs. Wages seasoning packet and simmering the sauce. The instructions on the packet say 20 minutes, but I usually try for more like 60 to 90 minutes to get a nice, thick sauce. While that is simmering, I am sterilizing the jars in the dishwasher and heating the rims and lids.

Once the dishwasher is done, the hot sauce goes in the hot jar/lid/rim, and gets turned upside down for five minutes to seal. I don't do the water bath thing for tomatoes anymore, and in the last ten years, I have only had a handful of jars go bad or not seal. After five minutes, turn the jars right side up and wait for the pings. LOVE those pings!

I don't know that we are saving any money by canning our own produce, but I do know that it tastes better from home, and I get such an immense sense of satisfaction at seeing all the jars lined up neatly on my pantry shelves for the winter.

On the flower gardening front, the mutant whiskey barrel of legend has done it once again. I am not sure that this is how large flowering kale is supposed to get, but it seems rather large to me!

While I am digging in all this dirt, I think about a recent news story about how good old farm dirt can actually increase a child's immunity. Well...DUH...all of us farm kids/parents have known this for decades. Did my kids play outside and get covered from head to toe with Lord knows what? You bet they did! In fact, I think Young Man took the cake on this one.

He couldn't have been more than 2 years old, and we were out in the barn visiting with Captain while he milked. At that time, we had a tie-stall barn which is where the cows are lined up on two sides, facing the outside walls, with a center walkway for the humans. The cow area was separated from the people area by a deep trench called a gutter. Basically, that was the cows' toilet. It got cleaned out once a day, or two milkings' worth of...*stuff.*

Anyway, Young Man was tearing up and down in the center aisle, bundled up in his winter coat and snowpants, and the only way to get him to slow down at all was to give him a lollipop and tell him he couldn't run with it. Unfortunately, I didn't say anything about not walking with it. He toddled along, got too close to the edge of the gutter and went head first into the...*stuff.*

Captain was quick as a flash and got him by the waistband of his snow pants and hauled him out. *Stuff* was running out of both pant legs and one coat sleeve. He had the other arm raised triumphantly over his head with the lollipop still clean and intact! He'd managed to keep it out of the...*stuff.*

However, as good as farm dirt can be for a child's immunity, there are things on the farm that are extremely dangerous and harmful. Young Man wasn't so lucky after an exposure to moldy corn in a grain bin, and he ended up in the hospital for two days getting steroids, antibiotics, and nebulizer treatments. Thankfully, he recovered well but will always need to be extremely careful around grain dust to prevent another attack.

Captain maybe summed this issue up best when he said: "Dirt don't hurt."

"A tithe of everything from the land, whether grain from the soil or fruit from the trees, belongs to the Lord; it is holy to the Lord." Leviticus 27:30

IT ALL BEGAN IN A BARN

I promised to tell the story of how Captain and I met through 4-H and started dating.

When I was in 4-H, I was part of the dairy judging team. Not because I wanted to be or had any great aptitude for it, I was just old enough to drive Baby Brother to the practices because he DID like it and DID have an aptitude for it. Seriously, I was just along for the ride and the socialization.

For those who aren't familiar with dairy judging practices, a group of kids get together in someone's barn and look at several groups of four dairy cows and decide which one is best, which one is worst, and where the two other ones fall in the middle. I didn't mind that part so much because the top and bottom cows were usually fairly obvious, and the middle two...well that could go either way.

Being Miss No Aptitude, I judged the cows like I judged a lot of things back in that era...on the cute factor. Who had the cutest spot pattern, who had a funky marking on their hip...stuff like that. This is most likely why I never made the official judging team like Baby Brother and Captain did.

Well, that and the fact that I truly sucked at giving oral reasons to the coach. Judging didn't just consist of picking out the order best-to-worst. You also had to be able to defend your reasons for making those choices, and "she had cuter spots" just didn't cut it for a good reason. I B.S.'ed my way through giving oral reasons to the coach most of the time, but neither one of us really ever had high expectations for me on that front.

So I was at practice one night and my eye happened to catch the cute factor. Not in the cows, but in this guy who was there. He'd been part of the dairy judging team and practices for years, but up to that night, he hadn't blipped on my radar.

Hmmm...must make conversation with him! So I casually (I hope) moseyed on over his way and heard him talking to his friend about a party. When I asked where the party was, I got an impish grin, an eye twinkle, and the response of "Wherever I am!" So modest is my man.

I grasped the opportunity to point out that Elgin Cheese Days was that coming weekend and I would be there solo...why didn't he just cruise on over and join the fun. So brazen I was!

He took me up on it, but the poor friend he brought with him ended up drinking by himself on the steps of the a local church while we were off...somewhere else.

That was all it took, and two weeks later we had our first official date. Somehow farming and cows have always been a part of our relationship from that first flirty episode at dairy judging, to date nights riding in tractors, to having a cow and bull on our wedding cake instead of the traditional bride and groom, to spending our honeymoon at the National FFA convention when he received the American Farmer Degree. But it all started in a barn with 4-H dairy judging.

Oh...the best part of the story. Almost forgot. After I bluffed my way through the oral reasons that night at practice with phrases like: More youthful udder, more angular at the withers, higher and wider in the thurls (I don't even know what that is), and more strength in the pasterns, the coach looked me straight in the eye and said it was the best set of reasons I'd ever done, and he was proud of me. I was on cloud nine with that for about five minutes...which is when I found out that I had judged the wrong four cows...epic fail. But--hey--I judged the right guy, didn't I?!?!

"He who finds a wife finds what is good and receives favor from the Lord." Proverbs 18:22

BOOK SMART, LIFE DUMB

There is a strong need for a study to be done on why a person cannot be blessed with both intelligence AND common sense. My theory is that during the course of creation, God decided that having both qualities would have caused circuit overload for most people, so He only allowed one trait or the other to be bestowed.

I am one of the unfortunate ones who got the book smarts instead of street/life smarts. This stood me in good stead during my 16-year academic career but hasn't been a whit of benefit since. I mean, I can balance the checkbook to the penny and SEE and ACKNOWLEDGE that corrective action is needed for the major deficit there. I just can't figure out what the action should be.

Luckily, I had the foresight—which is not the same as intelligence---to marry someone with common sense. Captain creatively (that's another word for common sense) steered us out of one financial fiasco with an utterly OBVIOUS solution: cutting up my cash card. I figured it was going to take extremely drastic measures…like the sale or rent of one of our children to someone not fortunate enough to have been blessed with offspring.

Mechanical problems and their associated difficulties are another area that is beyond my intellect. A flat tire during rush hour many years ago had me doing the 100-yard dash in high heels (this creates a bad mental image) to a phone booth to call Captain for some of his famous sage advice. Would you believe he actually suggested I change the tire myself? Not that I don't know how, because my daddy made sure I did. But there was no way I was going to squat down in high heels, which would hike my skirt to a nearly-illegal state, on the busiest street in town…not happening.

Sometimes, for inexplicable reasons, all cosmic mysteries are out in force at the same time and natural law is suspended, momentarily placing me at the upper end of the common sense scale. One such example is the time a doctor I worked for was saying that the last batch of cookies he'd made hadn't risen at all and ended up flat as pancakes. I asked him if he'd put baking powder in the dough, which I thought everyone knew was the ingredient that makes cookies rise (learned that in the 4-H foods project, by the way). With a puzzled look, he said, "No, I was out of that and since the recipe only called for ¼ teaspoon, I didn't think it was important." Dude, didn't you take chemistry in college or medical school?! Amazingly, we have remained good friends in the ensuing 24 years even though I was sort of a snot to him that day!

Another such example was the time Captain and his father were arguing about whether or not Captain should sell the straw bales he'd gotten from his oat crop (my father-in-law's viewpoint) or if the straw bales should go in the haymow to be used during the winter in case my father-in-law's supply ran short before spring (Captain's viewpoint). After listening to them—which is more than they were doing to each other, I might add—I suggested that Captain should sell the straw bales to his father, and then they would both be happy. To strike two people who are in the midst of a heated discussion completely dumb was enough to keep me happy for several days even though they didn't use my suggestion.

They say that opposites attract. Such is not the case for me. I was SMART enough to attract a sensible man, and he had the COMMON SENSE to get caught.

"In all your ways, acknowledge him, and he will make your paths straight." Proverbs 3:6

NATIONAL PRIDE

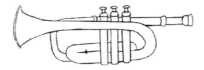

If you ever, for some odd reason, want to make me cry...play Taps. Just a couple of notes will do it. Every. Single. Time.

If I want to make you cry, I bet I could by telling you to YouTube "Taps history told by John Wayne." Go ahead, see if you can get through it dry-eyed.

Patriotism and national pride were big in our family when I was growing up. Dad served in the military as did two or three uncles and Big Brother. We always flew a flag during the day. Dad would raise the flag when he went out to milk in the morning, and at night when dusk approached, one of us would help him lower it and fold it. Pretty sure we can all, to this day, fold a flag in military precision. Guess whose job it was to run and lower the flag when a thunderstorm came up. *Gee, Dad, thanks for making me grab this metal pole amid flashes of lightning!!*

We were raised to stand for the flag during parades. There was never a question that during the national anthem we would face the flag with hands on our hearts, hats off, and *sing the words*.

What happened to that kind of respect? I have watched professional sports events, on television and in person, and many of those players don't sing or even mouth the words. They don't remove their hats. I just want to slap them. As much as they are getting paid, they can take two minutes and take their stupid hats off to respect the flag.

Do you remember where you were on September 11, 2001? Do you remember every single detail you heard about the airplanes flying into the Twin Towers? I was driving to work on Highway 14 from Byron to Rochester. I was on the phone with Captain telling him the guy at the elevator had been extremely rude to me when I dropped off our payment on my way to work. I heard the radio DJ say there was a news report that a plane hit the first tower.

I hung up with Captain, and listened in a jaded manner...thinking it was a spoof on some late night TV show skit from the night before. Then the DJ said a second plane hit the second tower, and I knew in that instant that there was something very serious going on. And I was scared.

As the details unfolded over the following days, there was a unity in this country that was unprecedented. What happened to that unity?

As we stop each year to remember, I'm sure I am not the only one who will shed a tear or two or many for those who lost their lives on 9/11. Moreover, I hope I am not the only one who will say a prayer for all those who **gave** their lives to help: military, law enforcement, firefighters, emergency medical staff, or ordinary people on a plane. And to all those who continue to serve our country to protect us, "Thank you, may God bless you always and keep you safe. Amen."

"Blessed is the nation whose God is the Lord, the people he chose for his inheritance." Psalms 33:12

CRAZY CROCHET LADY

I love September. It is my absolute favorite month of the year. Not just because Captain's birthday is that month, or our anniversary, or Cubby's birthday. I just love the way it looks, smells, and feels. In September I can enjoy being outdoors without it being too hot or cold. September is when harvest is gearing up, both in the garden and in the fields. Captain is busy outside with machine repair and maintenance, so he is a happy camper which makes me a happy camper.

Mostly I like September because the humidity is finally low enough that I can get back to my crochet projects. Trust me when I tell you that crocheting in July and August is not comfortable!

Crochet is another one of those things I sort of stumbled onto years ago. I used to do counted cross stitch until my eyesight finally got bad enough that it was hard to read the patterns and/or see the fabric well enough to do good work. I moved on to crochet because I knew knitting was out. Tried that as a kid and failed miserably. My grandma tried to teach me to tat when I was a kid, and that was a complete disaster. I did do macramé for a 4-H project when I was a kid, but there just isn't much call for macramé plant hangers anymore. That sort of went out in the 70s.

But who doesn't like a cozy blanket to curl up with on cold Minnesota winter nights?!

Doing crochet occupies my time in the evenings when I am watching TV while letting me create homemade gifts for all those fun milestone events like graduations, weddings, and babies. Plus, the best part is, if I make a mistake in the crochet pattern (and I do, invariably), no one is going to know unless I tell them because it is easy to mask by either adding or subtracting a stitch in the next row.

The first afghan I made was for our bed. The end result would have been the equivalent of a queen size comforter. I was maybe a dozen rows short of finishing it when, unfortunately, it went up in smoke when our house burned down. Tough luck. I have yet to make us a new blanket, now that I think about it. Huh.

I have oodles of resources for crochet stitches and patterns. However, being a creature of habit, I usually go to one of four of five favorite stitch patterns. I like patterns that keep it interesting such as the climbing shells stitch. If I don't keep the pattern interesting, I will get bored with it about six rows in and rip it all out to start over.

My second most favorite go-to stitch pattern is the chevron stitch, also known as a ripple stitch. This stitch looks great in multi-color yarns, one solid color yarn, or three or four rows of several different solid colors.

I tend to stick with an I-size hook because it is comfortable for my hand, and makes a nice, loose stitch. However, if I want to use a different size hook, I can do that because when Captain's Grandma Brogan passed on, I was given her collection of crochet hooks. It is nice to think that maybe some of his grandma's talent is transferring to me through the hooks. Or at least she knows that someone is carrying on with the craft that she enjoyed so much.

I also have WAY too much yarn. I am at the point where I almost need to install those shelves like they have in the yarn section at Hobby Lobby! Or maybe invest in more clear totes and dedicate one or two colors to each tote. Who knows?!

I love multi-color yarns because it gives me a unique color palette without having to switch colors every so many rows, which is a pain in the patoot. Sometimes I buy specific yarns for a particular recipient in mind, and sometimes I buy yarn just because it calls to me at Hobby Lobby. I've even seen yarn jump into my cart when I wasn't looking; or at least that is what I tell Captain when I come home with a dozen new skeins of yarn.

I only buy the Hobby Lobby store brand, I Love This Yarn, after the Great Unravel Incident of 2013. When a nephew got married a few years back, I ordered an afghan kit online which included that store's brand of yarn. I spent six months making their afghan, a lovely pattern of dark and light purple, dark and light olive green, and cream in a ripple pattern.

I always wash the afghans I make before I give them because I have been known to spill coffee or food on a project. When I washed the afghan for our nephew, two separate areas of the afghan unraveled in the washer leaving two monster-sized holes. Panic! This was just two or three weeks before their wedding which did not give me much time to make a different blanket, but I got it done. Different colors and different pattern, but still.

Captain took the unraveled blanket because he liked the fact it covered him up but he could stick his feet out the two holes and not get *too* hot. Never mind that I have made at least three different afghans specifically for him to curl up with that did not fall apart in the washer!

All I know is that with fall upon us, I am looking forward to several months of enjoyment wielding my crochet hook!

"Whatever your hand finds to do, do with your might; for there is no work or thought or knowledge or wisdom in Sheol, to which you are going." Ecclesiastes 9:10

NORTH SHORE TRIP – DAY 1

For the last several years, we have gone to the North Shore in September to celebrate our anniversary. I am not sure exactly what it is about Lake Superior and its shoreline that is so soothing. Is it the constant sound of the waves? Is it how the vastness of the lake makes any stress/worry/problem in my life seem inconsequential? Is it the pervasive smell of seagull poop? I don't know, and I really don't care. All I know is that it is something that I need for my inner self every year.

Most years we have reservations at a small resort in Little Marais about halfway up the shore called Superior Lakeside Cabins. This year...we had nothing. Part of that was because my vacation request at work wasn't finalized until the very last minute and part of it was because we just weren't sure what the crop was going to be doing and if Captain might be picking beans.

So Tuesday morning, we loaded up and headed out on a wing and a prayer that we wouldn't be sleeping in the truck for two nights. We sailed through the Cities just fine, but I am always glad Captain does the driving because I just can't handle interstate traffic through Saint Paul. It was truly a beautiful day for a drive with just a couple of stops at rest areas on I-35 and a lunch break at a KFC that offered a lunch buffet. Before we knew it, we were pulling into the rest area/information center just outside and above Duluth. That first look at the harbor and the lake always, always takes my breath away. After picking up some informational brochures, we headed into Duluth.

Some background information is needed here. Normally we would cruise through Duluth and head much further north where we would day trip from our cabin to the many state parks...Tettegouche, Cascade, Temperance River, Gooseberry Falls, and Split Rock. Sometimes we get really adventurous and go all the way to the Canadian border with a stop in Grand Marais. One of these years we will get passports so we can actually go **into** Canada instead of just looking at it from a distance. Anyhoo, this year, we approached the whole trip differently and decided to do the south end of the North Shore.

So in all the years we have been to the North Shore, we have only ever seen one boat come in off the lake, and that was 15 years ago. So many times we were just blowing through on our way further north and didn't have time to stop, or conversely, we were blowing through on our way home and didn't want to take the time to stop. Silly us!

So back to this year's trip. Captain had checked out the Duluth shipping news website and found that there would be a multitude of boats coming and going into Duluth during the three days that we would be there. As we were walking around at the Information Center, they had those telescope/binocular things that you pay a quarter to see way far away. Our investment of 25 cents showed us that, by cracky, there was a boat out in the lake headed for the canal.

So we boogied back to the truck and headed for Canal Park. Parking is always easy by the canal, so we snagged a spot close to the Army Corps of Engineer Museum on the canal. We had some time to walk clear out to the lighthouse at the end of the pier before the boat was getting close enough that they raised the lift bridge (plus a little sailboat was headed out to the lake). We walked halfway back down the pier for a good vantage point to watch the boat come in.

Folks, those things are HUGE! The one coming in on this particular day was in the upper 700-foot range, which is actually quite a bit smaller than the 1000-footers that often come in. But, it was still massive!

With that excitement behind us, we jumped back in the truck and headed out of town. We decided to take the old Scenic Highway between Duluth and Two Harbors instead of our normal choice of the Expressway. Yeah, bad idea. There was construction going on, and I am pretty sure we were driving in an area where the road was actually closed. But we made it to Two Harbors just fine. We saw that the tourist info office was open for business, so we pulled in to ask about lodging options.

The very nice lady working in the office told us that she had just taken calls from two resorts near Gooseberry Falls and that they had openings, one reasonable and one sort of high-end. She very kindly starred their names in the guidebook she gave us. She also had helpful information on dining choices within a 20-minute drive. We thanked her and headed back on the road.

This particular point of the trip is fairly typical of showcasing how polar opposite Captain and I are in our approach to things. I like to KNOW stuff; Captain is more of a wait-and-see kinda guy. His choice was *let's just drive and see what we see.* My choice was (because that sleeping in the back of the truck thing was lurking in my mind) *hey, let's use this new-fangled contraption called the cell phone and call these people!*

We sort of compromised. When we got to the turn off for the less expensive of the two options, their sign said "no vacancy." This seemed quite odd to me since it hadn't been a full half hour since they had called the tourist info office and told them they had an opening. So we pulled onto the frontage road and called them to double check.

Why yes, they did have a cabin available for the next two nights! Seeing as how we were about 45 seconds away, this worked out well. While I was jumping up and down in my seat with excitement because I wouldn't have to sleep in the truck, Captain asks what the price was. Huh...I never asked because--hey--I didn't care! Again, a spotlight on our oppositeness. Captain never seems to grasp the concept that I plan for these trips and set money aside every payday to cover the cost, and I try very hard to figure expenses on the high side so that I am sure we have enough funds. Thus, it didn't matter what it cost (and I was pretty sure it was going to be in our budget) AND it would save me from sleeping in the truck.

I probably shouldn't keep saying we'd sleep in the truck, as I am quite positive that there would have been motel choices further up the road, but I didn't want to stay in a dang hotel. I wanted to be ON THE LAKE, and I was willing to pay a little extra money for that luxury. So there!

Regardless, we had the cabin and it was just the cutest little thing ever! The only drawback of the cabin is that there was no TV. This is somewhat of a crisis for Captain, as (a) he is a newshound and starts jonesing if he goes more than 12 hours without a news broadcast and (b) he likes to fall asleep to the TV. Suck it up Bunky, you'll live.

After we got settled in, we realized we were going to need some supplies, such as coffee for morning. If I don't have coffee in the morning, people can get hurt. Plus, we needed some supper. We hit the grocery store in Silver Bay (20 miles north) for munchies, coffee, and beverages. Quick stop back at the cabin to unload those and then headed to Two Harbors to find food. As we were heading back that way, we were passed by The Little Old Lady From Pasadena. I kid you not! This woman had to be 90 years old, and she was INTENSE. Steering wheel gripped at 10 and 2, eyes straight ahead, and gas pedal smashed to the floor. She FLEW by us! Made me laugh right out loud.

By luck and happenstance, when we were driving around in Two Harbors, we stumbled across the Castle Danger Brewery. Captain is always up for trying new beer so we stopped. We had the nicest conversation with the bartender/owner! I am not a beer drinker by nature so I wasn't sure this was going to be fun for me, but I explained that to the barkeep and he recommended one of their more mild lagers for me. Good choice! I would actually drink that again, but probably not any time soon. Captain, on the other hand, likes the darker beers such as Guinness. First, he tried the second strongest lager they had, which he liked. Then the bartender talked him into trying their stout, which he said put Guinness to shame. All I remember from the description on the menu was that there was a hint of licorice in it. That just doesn't sound good to me, and I *like* licorice!

He pulled the tap to fill the glass, and it was black as pitch, my friends, with a lot of foam. He set the glass in front of Captain, who instantly went to take a drink. Barkeep and I both told him to wait for the foam to settle down a little bit first. A few seconds later, he took his sip and completely agreed that it was superior to Guinness. I tried a sip of it and let me tell you, I wouldn't drink that unless I hadn't had anything else to drink for days and was on the point of death. And then I would still probably think twice. Give me top shelf whiskey any day! But Captain liked it so all was well.

On to supper, and on the advice of our friendly neighborhood barkeep, we tried the Irish Pub down the street. We always try to eat local versus chain when we are vacationing, and this place fit the bill nicely. I should have taken pictures of the interior, but I was too busy watching the Twins game on TV. It had a beautiful, old, hammered copper ceiling, exposed ductwork, and brick walls...just amazing character. Even better than that was the clientele. You could tell that this was THE neighborhood bar [insert "Cheers" theme song] because as we were sitting there, a couple came in and before they even got to their bar stools, the bartender had their drinks out and in front of them! Captain can relate to this because when he goes to our local saloon in Mantorville, they know he is going to want a mug o'Mich, please (kudos to Scott and Corinne). Love that kind of personal service!

There was one guy who came in who had to be at least 80 years old, walking with a cane, with a snow white beard down to his chest. He nursed his one beer, commiserated with his stool mates about the day's happenings, and meandered back out the door for home. Kinda cute, actually. I could picture him doing this every day, just getting out and mingling instead of moping at home. You go, my elderly friend!

So, with full tummies and happy hearts, we headed back to our home away from home to enjoy some adult beverages on the deck for an hour or so before heading to bed. We opened the window facing the lake and drifted to sleep listening to the crash of the waves. It was the perfect ending to a pretty awesome day!

Stay tuned for Day 2's installment!

"Let the heavens be glad, and let the earth rejoice; let the sea roar, and all that fills it." Psalm 96:11

NORTH SHORE TRIP – DAY 2

The beginning of our second day started with an awesome sunrise over the lake. What better way to start the day! We enjoyed our coffee on the deck watching the sun come up over the lake and listening to the waves crash on the rocky shoreline just below the deck. We got cleaned up and dressed and spent some time exploring the shoreline. I finally, finally, finally got a picture of a wave actually crashing on the rocks! Been trying for that for five years.

After exploring the shoreline by the cabin, we headed out for a day of being tourists. First stop was Betty's Pies for breakfast (no pie, though). The original cafe had to move when the highway was rerouted/reconstructed, but they kept the original design and layout. Their history was written on the back of the menu, and in high summer season, they go through 350 to 400 handmade pies per DAY!

From Betty's Pies we headed back into Duluth to take a harbor cruise on the Vista Fleet...also something we have never ever done in all the years we have been going to the North Shore. We just did the narrated tour (versus a pizza cruise or a dinner cruise) which lasted a little over an hour. We went out into the lake for a bit, got some history about the lakefront area, and then cruised back under the lift bridge and around to where the boats load and unload. We saw taconite being loaded, limestone, and we saw the CHS terminal which is huge. They can load 35,000 bushels of corn per hour into a boat, and it takes about 11 hours to load a boat full. Do the math...that's a lot of stinking corn! We stayed on the top (open) deck and ended up standing next to another couple and got to chatting. Turns out they were from Lake City and on their first trip to the North Shore. We dispensed some sage advice on places to go, things to see or do, and places to eat. Like we are experts or something?!?!

After disembarking, we headed south on 35 a little bit to Jay Cooke State Park. I really can't believe we never did any of this stuff on our other trips. What an amazing place! JCSP was one of President Roosevelt's CCC projects, including a suspension bridge across the St. Louis River. Due to severe flooding over the years, they have had to rebuild the bridge four different times, but have stayed true to the original CCC construction with stone and logs. The rock formations were what got to me...the way these massive pieces of slate or granite or whatever they were just got stacked up like playing cards or something was just awesome! We stopped at the park's information center and ended up having the nicest conversation with a couple from Minneapolis. We chatted with them about camping, kids, farming, and life in general for about a half an hour. I love meeting new people!

Jumped back in the car and headed back to Duluth to drive the Scenic Byway way up above Duluth. There were incredible scenic overlooks and one park with a 5-story tower that was donated by royalty from Sweden, I believe. Seriously cool stuff.

By now our breakfast at Betty's Pies had worn off and we were hungry and getting tired, so we headed north out of Duluth to Two Harbors. We found the pizza place our friendly neighborhood barkeep had recommended the night before--Do North Pizza. Just a little hole in the wall place, but amazing pizza! There was a kids' birthday party going on so we didn't hang out longer than needed.

Back at the cabin, we were enjoying a beverage on the deck, and I saw lights out on the lake. The boat we had seen departing Duluth when we were in that 5-story tower was cruising past! Trust me, it was cool.

I was pretty much wiped out by 8:30 and went to bed. Again, the window was open to the crash of waves and I drifted off to dreamland for the night.

"Let the field exult, and everything in it! Then shall all the trees of the forest sing for joy." Psalm 96:12

North Shore Trip - Day 3

Good morning from Lake Superior! It was a bittersweet morning, knowing we had to head back to reality. The sunrise over the lake was epic to watch because there was a bank of clouds moving in, and there was only a thin band of clear sky between the lake and the cloud bank. We watched the sun peek over the horizon, show itself just for a minute, and then disappear into the clouds. Who would think that just a matter of seconds could be so breathtaking?

When we were here last, a new and improved visitor center at Tettegouche had been under construction, so we wanted to drive up and see that before we went home. Unfortunately, being early birds, the gift shop and interpretive center were not open yet when we were there. Still, the new center was very impressive from what we were able to see in the lobby area before driving back to the cabin.

We got our stuff packed up and did the housekeeping thing...washed dishes, swept floors, and emptied garbage cans. One last sweep to make sure we didn't leave anything behind like a cell phone charger or a watch. We've done that before, so we always double and triple check.

We stopped at the office to return the cabin keys and say goodbye to the resort owners, and their dog, JJ. He is an Airedale, but when we had pulled in on Tuesday, I called him an Ayrshire....a dairy cow. Shows what my background is apparently!

The drive down to Duluth was hampered by downpours off and on...the kind that make you think maybe you should pull onto the shoulder and wait it out. Captain, however, is made of sterner stuff and continued driving. I'm always glad to have a chauffeur in these situations!

Once we got parked in Duluth and checked the boat schedule, we found we had a little over an hour before its arrival. Finding breakfast was somewhat of a challenge as it is the "off" season in Duluth and businesses open later. We finally found a little cafe open and got seated, but due to slow service, we almost missed the boat's arrival and actually ran the last few yards to the lift bridge to see it. Memo to me: "Don't run on a full stomach...it hurts!"

With not just a little regret, we waved goodbye to Duluth and the North Shore and headed south. While stopping at a rest area later, we saw that there were several state parks close by, and we decided to check a couple of them out.

Banning State Park had a lovely rapids area and an old quarry site which we did not have the time or energy to investigate this time around. Perhaps another day. Captain almost dropped in the drink when he was walking on some slippery rocks by the rapids, but he gained his footing and stayed dry. Whew!

Back on the road we thought we would try for St. Croix State Park. Little did we know, until it was too late to turn around, that it was WAY out in the boonies; nearly to the Minnesota-Wisconsin border. Our visit there was mostly drive in and drive out again, but at least we can say we were there. Our bucket list said "visit every state park," not actually explore each one. We like to give ourselves wiggle room on these things!

Unfortunately, our little side trip to St. Croix put us behind in our schedule and we ended up hitting the cities at 4:00...just in time for rush hour. Add to that the fact that the Highway 52 ramp at the Lafayette Bridge was closed and we missed the detour (who can read those signs fast enough to move three lanes in three seconds???) we ended up going across town on I-35. Friends, you could not pay me enough to live there and have to drive that every day (no offense, Big Brother). No way in hell.

Usually Captain and I can navigate and travel fairly well together, but that particular section of the trip...not so much. After much discussion and debate, we took the 494 exit off of 35 and then the Dodd Road/Highway 55 exit and fumbled our way back to Highway 52. It's always a relief to me when we pass the Koch Refinery because I know, by cracky, I can find my way home from there!

Due to side trips, rush hour traffic, and general headache, we called Young Man on the way home and asked him to feed Captain's one calf. It was a burden, I know, but Young Man stepped up and helped us out.

We always eagerly anticipate the annual trip "up nort" and we always thoroughly enjoy our R&R. But it is still awfully nice to come home again and sleep in our own bed!

Thank you, friends, for joining us on our trip this year. I hope you enjoyed it as much as I have enjoyed sharing it with you!

"The Lord is my shepherd, I shall not want. He makes me lie down in green pastures; he leads me beside still waters; he restores my soul. He leads me in right paths for his name's sake." Psalms 23:1-3

DON'T NAME YOUR FOOD

Having grown up on a dairy farm, I learned many, many moons ago to never, ever name an animal that might end up being your food someday. There is nothing more devastating than sitting down to a steak dinner with your parents and having your dad say, "Yep, old Rollie sure makes good eating" when Rollie was my pet! It put me off steaks for quite a few years, although I have gotten back on that wagon.

As the wife of a dairy farmer turned beef farmer, I have kept that lesson in the front of my mind. Interestingly, I also learned that I have amazing powers that can control whether a calf will live or die. All it takes is for me to look at a calf and say, "Ooooh, he is so cute!" and you can bet dollars to donuts that the calf will not survive longer than three more days. After a few such incidents, I decided that all of our calves are ugly as a mud fence in the rain, and I refrain from comment.

New lesson learned…not only don't name your food, don't comment on its looks or personality!

Animals that are allowed to be named on a farm are anything that won't end up in the food supply: cats, dogs, birds, donkeys, and horses all fall in this category. Cats especially are hard to name even (or maybe especially) when they are outdoor cats. We used to have the standard Whiskers, Purrty, Mama Kitty, and so on. Those got boring, and I tried to get creative such as with Oscar and Felix, our very own odd couple.

Sadly, Felix didn't survive an especially harsh winter, and Oscar ended up part of an even odder couple…our Lab-Rottweiler-Dalmatian mix farm dog named Dipstick. Either Oscar thought he was a dog, or Dipstick thought he was a cat. Unfortunately, Oscar got into something that disagreed with him and passed away during the night.

On a side note, Dipstick lives up to (or down to, depending on your viewpoint) his name. Young Man named him because his tail is white at the end…like someone dipped it in paint. This poor creature was doomed from birth. Having lost out on being cute or smart, he has only one redeeming trait and that is being able to maintain a speed of 40 mph for a quarter mile or more. Not something to really write home about. Captain insists if we had named him Einstein, he wouldn't be dumb as dirt, but I'm not entirely sure I believe that.

Young Man and Princess had kittens when they were in elementary school. Young Man named his Mashy (for mashed potatoes…his favorite food at the time) and Princess named hers Colonel (for unknown reasons). They each met an untimely demise in vehicle-versus-cat incidents. That was the end of indoor cats for us until just a year or so ago when Princess was gifted a kitten from some friends of ours, and she promptly named the kitty…Princess. Feline Princess was kind of a pain in the butt, but at least she had the cute factor going for her.

Human Princess was a college student at the time, so feline Princess stayed with us while her mistress was away during school terms. It then came to my attention that human Princess would not be taking feline Princess when she moved out of our house into her own apartment. This didn't bother me so much because I happened to like the cat, but Captain was not pleased. In the end, it did not matter how we felt about it because feline Princess took an unprovoked swipe at Cubby at Christmastime, so she was re-gifted to a friend's mother. They are getting along nicely, by the way.

Captain is more of a dog person, although he did complain when Young Man's house dog stayed here for a while after Young Man moved out. However, in Captain's defense, Young Man's house dog was kind of a pain in the butt. He was a mini Pomeranian named Chewy. We first interpreted this as a reference to his resemblance to that lovable character from Star Wars...Chewbacca. That theory lasted about two days until Chewy...chewed. Everything. Shoes, phone charger cords, Kleenexes, and scissor handles. He was lucky he had the cute factor going for him or he would have been keeping company with the Odd Couple outside! I am pleased to say that Chewy now lives with his rightful masters, Young Man and Mama Bear.

This dilemma of not naming farm animals only came to mind recently because we not only have a hog at the locker ready to pick up, but we loaded out a steer this morning for butcher. Bottom line is to never, ever name something that is part of the food chain; never comment on an animal's looks or personality; and to apparently be mindful when naming farm pets so as not to doom them to not living up to their potential.

"A good name is to be chosen rather than great riches, and favor is better than silver or gold." Proverbs 22:1

RURAL RUSH HOUR

Drivers are stupid. Not the drivers I know, but all the other drivers. The ones who are in such a stinking hurry that they choose to put not only their lives, but mine and everyone else's, in danger.

Like the dork I saw today on West Circle Drive near the history center. He was about three cars ahead of me in the left-hand south-bound lane. He decided to pass the car ahead of him, not in the right-hand lane like a sane, rational person. Nope, he crossed a double yellow line, on a hill, on a curve, *into* the northbound turn lane! And guess what? A mile later at the stop light...there he was, the same as the rest of us. He gained nothing by making such a rash and idiotic maneuver.

We've all seen it time and time again. People passing in no passing zones. People texting and driving. People fiddling with the radio. I saw a lady once putting on her make up driving on Highway 52. Yeah, that's intelligent. You won't live long, but you'll look good dead! Yeesh.

Given that drivers are stupid (present company excluded) on a good day, we have to be doubly cautious of them now during what we like to call Rural Rush Hour. This is when farmers are on the road--making an honest living, I might add--with tractors, trucks, and other large, slow moving equipment.

I know that I am actually preaching to the choir. You all know what I am talking about, but I ask you to please share this with everyone you know anyway. If we can prevent one accident, or worse, through public awareness, then our job is done.

We have seen everything stupid when it comes to rural rush hour. Captain doesn't lose his temper very often, although it is impressive when he does, but one time when I was riding with him to take a semi load of corn to Kasson, we turned at the bridge in Mantorville, which is on a hill/curve/no passing zone.

The idiot driver behind us couldn't wait the five or ten seconds it would have taken to get to a passing zone...he passed us right there. And into the path of an oncoming car. Captain let loose a string of swears that turned the air blue, and he laid on the air horn.

The idiot, of course, squeaked through and kept going. The poor driver in the other car had to use part of the ditch to avoid the collision. And I had to take a dozen deep breaths to get my heart rate back to normal.

We have had people pass us and we have been flipped off, yelled at, crowded onto the shoulder, and honked at. I know there are those of you out there that have had the same things happen. Don't you just want to hunt these fools down and stomp them stupid? Or, stupider, I guess.

Do farmers charge into board rooms on Wall Street and tell those yahoos to hurry it up? Nope. Then why does everyone else get to treat us so rudely as we go about our business? I really want to know!

Okay, choir of mine, let's sing it to the rafters and let everyone know that harvest time may involve some traffic delays. There is going to be some noise and dirt near towns and subdivisions. There is going to be dirt and other agriculture debris on the roadways.

But you know what? There is going to be abundant food on the grocery store shelves, the milk coolers in every Kwik Trip are going to be full to bursting, and there is going to be the safest and cheapest food in the world at our doorsteps.

I always pray for bountiful harvests, but more, I pray for safe harvests.

"The prudent see danger and take refuge, but the simple keep going and suffer for it." Proverbs 27:12

MY HOUSE WAS CLEAN LAST WEEK

I saw a wall hanging at Hobby Lobby one time that said, "My house was clean last week, sorry you missed it." This sums up my housecleaning creed. Martha Stewart I am not.

Many of my friends have immaculate homes. They move their furniture every week and vacuum under it. Personally, I move my furniture to *cover* the dirt. The only reasons for moving furniture are to locate a lost TV remote or to permanently vacate the premises.

I know people who wash their windows inside AND out—not biannually like I do—but quarterly. Imagine that! I try to claim that my windows are dirty because all the dust from the gravel road that runs past our house collects on the outside and just makes them *look* dirty. Thankfully, no one ever questioned why there were little hand prints on my windows back in the day.

When someone (usually Captain) catches on to my evasion tactics and suggests I actually clean the outside of the windows, I can delay the chore indefinitely by 1) claiming it's too cold outside or 2) claiming it's too warm outside. The second option always gave me the flexibility to claim parental quality time with my children because soon it would be too cold to play with them outside, or wash windows for that matter.

My sister-in-law is a cleaning fiend. This woman vacuums her heat registers several times each year. I had never heard of such a thing until I met her. After I heard about it, I decided it was a waste of time because when the furnace is turned on, it will blow the dirt out of the register and into more easily accessible places to be sucked up by the vacuum cleaner.

An old, proud saying of many women is, "You could eat off my floor." I can shamefully say this too. Princess used to sustain herself for two or three days with food she found on my floor. When she was spending a lot of time in her walker, I would give her Cheerios on her walker tray. She would get so excited and wave her hands so hard that Cheerios would fly everywhere. Several days later, I'd see her on her tummy reaching under the couch, pulling out those Cheerios for a snack.

Captain does not nag or scold about my less-than-sterling housekeeping. He is much more subtle than that. When I recently had the time, energy, and inclination to dust my bookcase because I was on a summer vacation day, I found a message written in the dust: January 17. I thought this was a date he wanted to remember, so I decided not to disturb it, thereby freeing myself from another dreaded household chore. I was quite deflated to learn that he had written that when he first noticed the dust piling up on the bookcase.

When well-intentioned people ask why I didn't have my children help me do some cleaning, I quickly recited the Phyllis Diller quote that holds so much truth: "Trying to clean your house while your children are growing is like trying to shovel your sidewalk while it's still snowing."

Case in point: When Young Man was about 5, I asked him to take his clean clothes upstairs and put them away. Now, "away"—even to my dust-shrouded mind—means *in the drawers*. Young Man interpreted "away" to mean "someplace else" and proceeded to transfer the clothes from the laundry room to the stairway. When I suggested he actually take the clothes upstairs and put them "away," he expanded his interpretation to mean "someplace else...where Mom can't see them." I found them all piled on top of the dresser. I didn't belabor my point; at least they were out of MY sight.

You have heard about homes that are decorated in an "early rustic" theme, right? MY basement is decorated in early cobweb. It would make a terrific spook house. I can just imagine the visitors to our hot new tourist attraction *ooohhhing* and *aaaahhhing* over the authentic props we used. This way I wouldn't have to spend time cleaning the basement AND I could guarantee enough income from my authentic spook house to actually pay for a maid. Of course, this would eliminate the income-generating spook house.

We have an open door policy around here, and we are happy to have company anytime...as long as you don't care what state of cleanliness we are at. I will always be able to find a clean coffee cup for you to use, and we'll have a nice visit. My policy has always been, and will always be: If you are coming to see me, come anytime. If you are coming to see my house, make an appointment.

"By wisdom a house is built, and through understanding, it is established." Proverbs 24:3

ABOUT THE ILLUSTRATOR

Brianna Quintero was born and raised in Minnesota. She is an illustrator, specializing in character design at the Minneapolis College of Art and Design. *Misdeeds by the Misguided* is her first book illustration. Brianna can be contacted at bqbungert@yahoo.com.

ABOUT THE AUTHOR

Jude Brogan grew up on a dairy farm in Southeastern Minnesota. She completed her bachelor's degree in Communications at Andrew Jackson University in Birmingham, Alabama, and did a stint as a free-lance writer. She is married to a farmer, raised two children, gained a daughter-in-law, and has one adorable granddaughter. She cares deeply for her family and friends and is involved in her community. She supports the 4-H and FFA programs and has a passion for writing, reading, crocheting, and gardening.

Jude writes a blog, "Misdeeds by the Misguided," which is the basis for this book. It is a look into the life and times of an everyday farm wife who likes writing, reading, crocheting, photography, cooking/canning, and camping. See the triumphs (few) and failures (many) of Jude. Meet Captain (husband), Young Man (son), Princess (daughter), Mama Bear (daughter-in-law), and Cubby (granddaughter). Grab your favorite beverage and enjoy a visit to her blog at https://misdeedsbythemisguided.blogspot.com.

Be sure to like Misdeeds by the Misguided on Facebook!

Made in the USA
Lexington, KY
15 November 2017